THE WAY IT WAS...

COMING OF AGE IN HARRISONBURG, VIRGINIA IN THE JIM CROW ERA

THE MEMOIRS OF DORIS HARPER ALLEN

Edited by Mark Metzler Sawin
With Billo Harper & the Harper Family

The Way It Was…

Coming of Age in Harrisonburg, Virginia in the Jim Crow Era

The Memoirs of Doris Harper Allen

Edited by Mark Metzler Sawin
with Billo Harper & the Harper Family

Published by the Estate of Doris Harper Allen
Harrisonburg, Virginia
2023

The Way It Was… Coming of Age in Harrisonburg, Virginia in the Jim Crow Era. The Memoirs of Doris Harper Allen / Doris Harper Allen edited with essays by Mark Metzler Sawin

This edition of Doris Harper Allen's Memoirs, including all notes and photographs copyright © William "Billo" Harper & the Harper Family
Essays copyright © Mark Metzler Sawin
ALL RIGHTS RESERVED
2023

Library of Congress Control Number: 2023901264

ISBN: 9798373664486

Library of Congress Cataloging-in-Publication Data

Doris Harper Allen, 1927–2021
Mark Metzler Sawin, 1970–
The Way It Was… Coming of Age in Harrisonburg, Virginia in the Jim Crow Era. The Memoirs of Doris Harper Allen—
ISBN 9798373664486 (pbk)

Praise of
Dr. Doris Harper Allen's Work

To many, she was Miss Doris; to me, Aunt. The last of the three Howard Sisters, and if you knew the Howard Sisters, they were unique in their way, and it is no surprise that Aunt Doris was the FIRE. She was more than an AUNT to us-she was our lifeline. She held us all together. She knew all of our birthdays; she was there for all of our special events; she was there when we were sick, grieving, married, divorced, you name it. Doris Allen was there. She showed us how to live life to the fullest. I often talk about Aunt Doris in my speeches because she taught me how to be a servant leader and serve my community. She taught me to have no fear; she taught me how to be noisy and put myself at the table.

Because of her fearlessness, I dared to run for public office. My Aunt Doris was tenacious. In her 80s, she wrote her first book, *The Way it Was Not The Way It Is*, and in her 90s, she wrote her second book, *Jim Crow in 30s, 40s, 50s and 60s; What was life like living in Harrisonburg Virginia and the Shenandoah Valley*. The Memories of Doris Harper Allen is the unbossed, unbought, unapologetic voice of Doris Harper Allen. Doris Jean Howard Harper Allen, Doctor, Author, Activist, Trailblazer, Mentor, Eastern Star, and Woman of God, thank you for your voice.

Love you, Auntie! Your legacy lives on.
Deanna Reed
Mayor, Harrisonburg, Virginia

Dr. Doris Allen Harper in life mentored many people and organization on how to improve the status of families and communities. She ministered on earth, as I experienced; was to improve the quality of life for all citizens regardless of their gender or color.

Dr. Harper mentored me and shared her wisdom to ensure that the needs of the local communities in Harrisonburg were identified. She focused on the youth and the elderly vulnerability in Huntington, West Virginia and Harrisonburg, Virginia for many years and leaves a legacy in both cities and states.

Dr. Harper would have personal conversations with me by phone or in person to inspire and encourage the elected officials to improve our communities in safety and employment. She often reminded me that been a leader, often you stand by yourself but always know that God is in the upper room, and he will give you what you need to take care of his people.

Although Dr. Doris Allen Harper could not attend Madison College because of Jim Crow Laws before, Dr. Allen went to the upper room to be with her God, she was able to see the building with her name Dr. Doris Allen Harper, on the Campus of James Madison University.

> With much love and respect!
> Larry M. Rogers
> Former Mayor, Harrisonburg Va.

CONTENTS

Note on Text & Photographs ... *xi*

Remembering My Mother, The Unapologetic Community Activist
  By Billo Harper ... *1*

The World of Doris Harper Allen
  An Essay by Mark Metzler Sawin ... *11*

The Way it Was…
  The Memoirs of Doris Harper Allen ... *41*

Maps ... *179*

Acknowledgements ... *183*

Newtown, Mennonites & the 1939 Gay St. Mission Photograph
  By Mark Metzler Sawin ... *195*

Appendices ... *205*

Note on Text

In 2015, Doris Harper Allen first recorded her memories in a self-published book entitled *The Way It Was Not the Way It Is*. She then produced a second manuscript with the working title, *Jim Crow in the 30s, 40s, 50s, and 60s: What Was Life Really Like Living Under Jim Crow Laws in Harrisonburg Virginia and the Shenandoah Valley?*, publishing a preliminary version in the months before she had a stroke in 2019. The text presented here is a synthesis of these two works, along with some of her other writings, restructured into a chronological and thematic order. Slight editing for clarity and notes to provide context have been added, but the unique and powerful voice of Doris Harper Allen are primary—her wit, wisdom, words, and style are what make this text the lively and insightful read that it is.

– Mark Metzler Sawin

Note on Photographs

Unless otherwise specified, all images in this book come from the Harper family and were provided by Doris Harper Allen and her family and digitized by her son, Billo Harper.

*The "Three B's": Doris Harper Allen's children,
Belinda (b.1950), Robert "Bob" (b.1951), and William "Billo" (b.1953)*

Remembering My Mother, The Unapologetic Community Activist
By Billo Harper

My mother, Dr. Doris Harper Allen over many years talked about how black people could get better results through education. We must exercise "the right to vote" is what she lived by. She loved Fannie Lou Hammer who brought voting and the civil rights struggle to Mississippi. Ms. Hammer led a delegation to the National Democratic Convention in 1964. My mother lived by one of her quotes "I'm sick and tired of being sick and tired." Even though civil rights made progress, we have a responsibility based on common challenges in today's America to support each other because of mutual interests that can create a better society for all. She used to always tell me after our personal debates between a mother and her son, "stop blaming others and the systems for your dysfunctional life," "take responsibility," and "you can change the systems you believe in, if you are willing to work."

Her life as a community activist in Harrisonburg, Virginia and Huntington, West Virginia is epitomized by one of my favorite speeches—Frederick Douglass's "What the Black Man Wants." Given in 1865 at the Annual Meeting of the Massachusetts Anti-Slavery Society, just days before the end of the Civil War, Douglass proclaimed:

> I hold that that policy is our chief danger at the present moment; that it practically enslaves the Negro and makes the [Emancipation] Proclamation of 1863 a mockery and delusion. What is freedom? It is the right to choose one's own employment.

I am a student of history and my mother's legacy to me is recognizing how her community and family didn't allow for Jim Crow to stop them from living out their family values and working toward the success of the collective. My mother worked as a maid for a prominent White Harrisonburg family, helping to raise their children while raising her own family as well. Octavia Spencer and Viola Davis in the film "The Help" captured her reality. Corey Harris, an American Blues Musician and MacArthur Genius Awardee, provided pointed lyrics from his song called "Maggie Walker Blues" which capture the true struggle and entrepreneurial spirit that black women endure and live, while still raising their own family, running a business, and making an impact doing good in their community.

My mother's first book, *The Way It Was Not the Way It Is* (2015) was her foundation and understanding of being born black and raised in a segregated Harrisonburg, VA during the 1930s, 40s, and 50s in the community called Newtown "where the blacks lived." She completed her final draft, after four different editors and writing challenges that included the process of being an 87-year-old self-published author, researching at James Madison University's Carrier Library, and choosing personal photos from her collections of photos taken with her brownie camera that her father Leo Howard purchased for her as a teenager in 1940.

Having one of the first cameras in the community was unique, and her getting it was a personal acknowledgement by her dad of her adolescent talent—a significant understanding during Jim Crow. Using this Brownie camera, developed by George Eastman as a simple point and capture camera, allowed her to document the Howard and Harper families as well as the Newtown community's history. Now we have the evolution of smart phone technology that supports our world of social media content creators in 2023. We often forget how rare images like those she made were in her times nearly one hundred years ago. Her design and creative abilities continued thru life and allowed her to design the cover of her first book cover. It was a joy to support her writing her first book, *The Way It Was Not the Way It Is*. During the process there were personal disagreements about design (and our positions, recommendations, and opinions lost out most of the time!), because her personality was one of insightfulness and candor. This was something her mother, father, brothers, sisters, nieces, nephews, and the three B's (her children Belinda, Bob, and Bill), and her close friends all knew. She would have success and some failures as a writer, but all decisions would be based on her final opinion. She would say, "My son the struggle in on going but the blessings keep right on flowing. As James Cleveland says, "I Don't Feel No Ways Tired."

My main goal working with my mother at the start of writing her first book was to see it completed in her lifetime. We together accomplished that goal. We didn't know she had another book in mind—it was a surprise to my brother, sister and me, and it concerned us all when it was about her Jim Crow experience, growing up in the South close to the Confederate Battlefield of New Market, Virginia. She started doing her own research around the Shenandoah Valley and across the internet, and she was constantly sending emails to local historians about the Confederacy and researching to get her facts correct. It was so inspiriting to see her at 86 years of life organizing her living environment to accommodate producing both of her books. She was a graduate of Lucy F. Simms School in 1947, a school build in 1939 as one of Franklin D. Roosevelt's Works Progress Administration projects during the Great Depression. Her educational foundation was provided by master instructor and legendary educator Ms. Lucy F. Simms (who attended Hampton University during the same time as Booker T. Washington), who taught her at the Effinger Street School in first and second grade, in which she made the honor roll. The school had many other distinguish teachers who followed the legacy of Ms. Lucy F. Simms, like Mary A. (Awkard) Fairfax and the NASA genius, Dr.

David R. Hedgley who taught science at Simms and later became inventor and designer of 3-D graphics used by computers today.

Her second book was called *Jim Crow in 30s, 40s, 50s and 60s; What was life really like living under Jim Crow Laws in Harrisonburg Virginia and the Shenandoah Valley*, and was a complete surprise and a sign of the tumultuous times we currently live in. It provided a local history of what black life was like here in Harrisonburg in another time. She provided a needed lens to *Brown vs Board of Education* and I am proud to see Congressman Bobby Scott of the Commonwealth of Virginia recognizing the need for our United States Congress to address its legacy by representation of a Bill to invest in Virginia Schools from disadvantage communities in the Commonwealth.

Once *The Way It Was. Not the Way It Is* was printed in 2015, she moved right into her life of being an entrepreneur. She did book signings, had many private conversations over the phone and in person, and as an 88-year-old elder traveled throughout the Shenandoah Valley selling her books, with boxes of books in the trunk of her car and setting up her own tables at Red Front grocery store and at the Lucy F. Simms Continuing Education Center in Harrisonburg. It was amazing to see and experience such an entrepreneurial mother! When President Obama ran for office, I still remember her calling me in Maryland and asking me if I could go to DC and get her some Obama Buttons—she wanted to sell them to make money to off-set her fixed retiree income. She said, "Folks in Virginia don't believe he can beat Hillary Clinton, but son trust me he can do it." Her insight was remarkable. I recalled how she and our community loved James Brown "Say It Loud I'm Black and Proud" which speaks to black empowerment and self-reliance:

> I've worked on jobs with my feet and my hands
> But all the work I did was for the other man
> And now we demand a chance
> To do things for ourselves
> We're tired of beating our heads against the wall
> And working for someone else.

The life she lived working for white families as a maid while having the responsibility to support and raise her own children was always a challenge to accept and understand for me. As a black youth growing up in the 1950–1960s in Harrisonburg, VA we had to sit in the balcony of the Virginia Theatre on main street because of Jim Crow.

During her many years living in Huntington, WV she gained a lot of knowledge and experience in community empowerment— efforts that even resulted in her meeting Muhammad Ali! Her leadership example always was "be You," and, "Stand up to society for what you believe in." When she retired and moved from West Virginia back to her childhood home of Harrisonburg, VA in 1997, she brought all this experience with her and continued working as a community organizer.

My technology company provided her at age 77 with her first computer that supported her love of technology and aided her with writing her memoirs. The Virginia Mennonite Retirement Center's computer lab was her home office when her apartment computer was down. Her emails daily to friends and associates was a challenge she welcomed— she reached out to family members for technical support often. The patience she demonstrated most of the time was a lesson for all of us as we get older—we should all be prepared to embrace being patient when embarking on new experiences of using technology. Some of the emails she wrote over the years for those who received them where short, using abbreviated words even before Twitter! It was effective writing with clarity... if you could understand her D.H. Allen style! She mastered the constraints of the written word and at 86-years-old was finally becoming a self-published author. That brought her extraordinary satisfaction. It reminded me recently of the great works of Lorraine Hansberry like "A Raisin in the Sun" that came to Broadway in 1959 and was later both a film starring Sidney Poitier and a show launched by Hip-Hop icon Sean Puffy Combs on Broadway. Hansberry's unique interviews were recently captured by James Madison University professor Mollie Godfrey in her book, *Conversations with Lorraine Hansberry*.

Mama grew up in Newtown in the Northeast section of Harrisonburg during the 1930s, 40s, and 50s, and because she was black, she wasn't allowed to attend Madison College, now called James Madison University, named after James Madison, the author of the American Constitution and the fourth president of the United States of America. But years later, in 2021 after extensive evaluation and review, a JMU history committee selected her along with fellow African American leaders Drs. Joanne V. and Alexander Gabbin, Dr. Sheary Darcus Johnson, and Robert Walker Lee, to receive buildings named in their honor. Her building, formerly named for the Confederate general Turner Ashby, is now called the Harper Allen-Lee Hall, and sits prominently on JMU's historic quad.

Mama understood we live on earth a short time. The community you live in requires you as a resident to be of service to those in need. Every Sunday morning, she would travel throughout the community picking up kids to attend Sunday school at our John Wesley Methodist Church, located in downtown Harrisonburg, VA. It was the only black-owned building downtown during the Jim Crow era and today would have been a historical landmark. But in the 1950s, city officials applied political pressure to convince the African American church members to sell the building to Westsel Seed Company, the Shenandoah Valley' first seed, feed, and plant business. The City of Harrisonburg's plan was to move our church to the northeast section of town where most black people lived. It divided the church membership. This was the start of urban renewal and land resettlement, which destroyed the northeast black community and the many black businesses that had formed during Jim Crow.

Having my mother finish writing two books at the age of 91, was inspiring. In America today more than ever is the time for black people to be more successful in community development and to create new business ownership as entrepreneurs. We must be sure not to allow the challenges of inadequate financial resources to hold us back from success. If you embrace education and keep your focus supported by discipline, you can win.

In 1963 she and my brother Robert Harper travelled in the back of a bus as the only blacks from Harrisonburg to Washington, DC to attend the "March on Washington for Jobs and Freedom" and heard Dr. Martin Luther King's historic "I Have a Dream" speech live and in person.

So now, let me introduce you to her new edited and insightful book memoirs that includes an introduction from my good friend Professor Mark Metzler Sawin, Professor of History and Honors at Eastern Mennonite University. It was his original idea which we both collaborated on to combine both books to provided students and teachers of local and national American history a valuable lens thru MaMa's unique memoirs of how she navigated within her community to provide authentic leadership and service. His enhanced editorial approach to Dr. Doris Harper Allen's memoirs was appreciated by our family, friends, colleague, and associates. His historical reference and context to the Jim Crow era, Harlem Renaissance, and to the Civil Rights Movement was distinct and gives real substance to her story of growing up, starting a family, and becoming a community organizer and activist in the Shenandoah Valley. It was always the goal of my mother that her story would be an easy read for students someday, and that teachers could incorporate her books in their curriculum designs.

You will enjoy this enhanced editorial approach by an historian who comes from the Midwest of America. Mark and his students were befriended various times by Mama who graciously and enthusiastically told them her life stories about "Newtown" on personal tours in the Northeast Neighborhood of Harrisonburg. She vividly explained the joys of community living "back in the day" and her examples of living a life of service to others in the beautiful Shenandoah Valley.

A bonus in this volume includes going inside her belief, love, and relationship with Mennonite fellowship and culture. I am sure you will be inspired upon reading this new edited version that combines both of her amazing books and introductions, and her experiences with the Gay Street Mennonite Mission in Harrisonburg, starting in 1939 when she was 12-years-old.

Mama was an original and authentic example of community organizing, leadership, spirituality, and services to others in need. These lyrics to Gregory Porter's classic song, "Take me to the Alley" represents how Mama in Huntington, West Virginia during the 1970s would go to "the Alley" on Saturday mornings with her personally cooked beans and cornbread to feed the homeless.

>Take me to the alley
>Take me to the afflicted ones
>Take me to the lonely ones that somehow
>Lost their way
>Let them hear me say
>I am your friend
>Come to my table
>Rest here in my garden
>You will have pardon

>Givethanx!

>WillieDell (*the name Mama called me, after my Granddaddy Bill and Grandmama Della*)

I Givethanx to Sylvia Louise Quinton
for her legal insight and genuine friendship to MaMa.

I Givethanx to P. Thandi Hicks Harper
for her unconditional support of MaMa's written works and being a true advocate of her legacy for social justice. Your scholarship was my road map to finally complete this book.

And finally…

To my sister Belinda and my brother Bob, MaMa kept us together and we are still together. Givethanx for being The Best Sister and Brother in the World…Love You Both 4 ever. Little Bro.

The "Three Bs"
Bob, Belinda, & Billo

In 1963

and in

2015 with their mother as she sold copies of her first book at the Simms Center

Doris (Howard) Harper Allen (c. 1945)

The World of Doris Harper Allen
By Mark Metzler Sawin

During James Madison University's 2019 graduation ceremony, special time was carved out to allow president Jonathan R. Alger to award Doris Harper Allen an honorary doctoral degree. He explained that such a degree was a just honor and long-overdue, for Harper Allen, like all other African Americans who had applied to JMU in the Jim Crow era, was unjustly denied admission. But Harper Allen had persisted. Denied admission as a student, she instead went to work as a cook for the school's president to gain economic resources while also raising a family and investing heavily in her community, constantly pushing for an end to segregation and better educational options for all of Harrisonburg's children, black and white. Later in life, she took courses at Marshall University in Huntington, WV, where she also worked and organized for issues of racial and gender equality for nearly thirty years. In his remarks, Alger noted that, "Fortunately for all of us here," in her later years, "Ms. Allen returned to Harrisonburg and continued her commitment as a community leader." He explained that besides writing about her life amidst the challenges of Jim Crow, she had also been "deeply involved in revitalization efforts in the Northeast neighborhood" and that she was "a critical voice in the renaming of Martin Luther King Jr. Way," a street that boarders JMU's campus.[1]

---

[1] The full text of President Alger's remarks during the doctoral award for Doris Harper Allen can be found in the appendices at the end of this book.

This was not the only recognition the community bestowed upon Doris Harper Allen. Amidst the racial reckoning that swept the nation in the aftermath of the police murders of George Floyd and Breonna Taylor in 2020, JMU removed the names of Confederate politicians and generals from three prominent buildings on its main quad, and in February of 2021, the university renamed them for African American individuals significant to its history. One of these buildings, an historic residence hall constructed in 1911, was renamed Harper Allen-Lee Hall in recognition of Robert Walker Lee, JMU's first black employee, and Doris Harper Allen. In making this announcement, Alger explained that this renaming was important because it sent "a powerful message that the university is evolving." This sort of change was exactly what Harper Allen had pushed for since she was first denied admission to JMU. As Alger noted, "We should be a better and stronger and more inclusive and more welcoming university as time goes on." JMU's student newspaper, *The Breeze*, ran a story about the renaming of Harper Allen-Lee Hall on March 4, 2021—auspicious timing given that on that same day, Doris Harper Allen passed away, having spent more than 93 years living and working for racial justice and equality in Harrisonburg, Virginia.[2]

What follows are the words and stories of Doris Harper Allen—accounts of what day-to-day life was like for the proud and strong African American community of "Newtown" that was intimately connected to, but strictly segregated from, the white

---

[2] See Eda Tercan, "JMU community reacts to Quad building name changes," *The Breeze* (March 4, 2021), Available at: www.breezejmu.org/news/jmu-community-reacts-to-quad-building-name-changes/article_7668eff8-7c6a-11eb-b47d-57c10ba54883.html. For Doris Harper Allen's obituary see "NAACP: Harrisonburg 'Trailblazer' Doris Harper Allen Dies," *Daily News-Record* (Harrisonburg, VA: March 7, 2021), Available at: www.dnronline.com/news/naacp-harrisonburg-trailblazer-doris-harper-allen-dies/article_e0f5e41f-2743-5694-bcd2-2629fbd2fab3.html.

residents of Harrisonburg, Virginia. Harper Allen first recorded her memories in a self-published book entitled *The Way It Was Not the Way It Is* in 2015. She then produced a second manuscript with the working title, *Jim Crow in the 30s, 40s, 50s, and 60s: What Was Life Really Like Living Under Jim Crow Laws in Harrisonburg Virginia and the Shenandoah Valley?*, publishing a preliminary version in the months before she had a stroke in 2019. In both these efforts Harper Allen also worked closely with two other local women who served as her editors but who also became close friends: Esther Stenson a local Mennonite writer and educator, and Robin Lyttle who was one of the founders of the Shenandoah Valley Black Heritage Project. In the last years of her life, Harper Allen and her family had the vision of turning these two accounts into a resource for the community as a whole, but especially for teachers and students, in an effort to educate the next generation and thus promote a better, more-just, and equitable future for everyone.

In 2001, about the same time Doris Harper Allen moved back to Harrisonburg from West Virginia, I moved to the community as well, taking a job teaching U.S. history at Eastern Mennonite University. Over the years that followed, Ms. Harper Allen took me under her wing time and again, providing me and my students important lessons about the realities, resourcefulness, and resilience of the citizens of Newtown. I was thus pleased and honored when Dr. Harper Allen's son, William "Billo" Harper, approached me about editing her manuscripts together into a combined resource for teachers, students, and the public. The text below is a synthesis of her writings, and this introduction will, I hope, provide some context for understanding the importance of her life and the life of the Newtown community.

Doris Harper Allen was born on September 28, 1927 and christened Doris Jean Howard, the fourth child of Leo and Julia (Hughes) Howard. 1927 was a dynamic and eventful year in the United States as the economy was booming and new "modern" conveniences were all the rage as many consumer goods reached the American public for the first time. The nation's houses became increasingly equipped with conveniences we now take for granted—things like electricity, indoor plumbing, and the telephone began to become part of daily life.

1927 was also the year Charles Lindberg flew the first solo flight across the Atlantic Ocean, and that Columbia Phonographic Broadcasting System first went on the air with 47 radio stations, launching what would eventually become CBS. Films moved from silent to "talkies" that year as well with the release of Al Jolson's *The Jazz Singer* in which Jolson, a white performer, dawned blackface, and in the hugely racist and exaggerated style of vaudeville, sang the song, "My Mammy," to great acclaim. That year in sports, in the entirely segregated Major League Baseball, the Yankee's famous "Murderer's Row" that included Babe Ruth and Lou Gehrig swept the world series in just four games—they didn't have to face Satchel Paige, who was then just finishing the first-year of what would become an astounding 39-year professional baseball career in the Negro Leagues and then in the MLB when desegregation efforts finally allowed him to compete in 1948. In 1927 African American music and culture were also flourishing amidst the Harlem Renaissance, turning black culture into the primary driver of all American culture in the "Jazz Age." Louis Armstrong and his Hot Seven formed, recording "West End Blues" the next year that revolutionized the world of Jazz; Duke Ellington's "Jungle Music" was heard across the nation, broadcast from the Cotton Club in Harlem where Ellington and his all-black band were hugely popular among its largely white-only audiences; and Bessie Smith's huge blues voice rang across the nation with the release of her hit blues record, "Alexander's Ragtime Band."

In literature, African Americans were also making their mark as the year before writers such as Claude McKay, Wallace Thurman, Countee Cullen, Zora Neale Hurston, and Langston Hughes burst onto the scene with their strong, unapologetic voices via their own literary magazine, *Fire!!* In his essay "The Negro Artist and the Racial Mountain" published in *The Nation*, Langston Hughes explained this new literary phenomenon, saying:

> The younger Negro artists who create now intend to express our individual dark-skinned selves without fear or shame. If white people are pleased we are glad. If they are not, it doesn't matter. We know we are beautiful. And ugly, too. The tom-tom cries, and the tom-tom laughs. If colored people are pleased we are glad. If they are not, their displeasure doesn't matter either. We build our temples for tomorrow, strong as we know how, and we stand on top of the mountain free within ourselves.[3]

This liberated spirit of the "New Negro" also drove the National Association for the Advancement of Colored People (NAACP) which, thanks to the leadership of W.E.B. DuBois and James Weldon Johnson, had become a powerful organization, working hard to counteract the "separate but equal" reality established by the Supreme Court's 1896 *Plessy v Ferguson* ruling that legalized racial segregation.

Though African Americans had much to be proud and optimistic about in 1927, they were also experiencing major pushback from an unapologetically racist white society. Marcus Garvey and his Universal Negro Improvement Association had come from Jamaica and burst onto the scene in Harlem in the 1910s, providing over a thousand jobs via its black-owned stores and strong social and civic organizations. But Garvey's powerful influence and constant call for black pride and power (his slogan was "Up you Mighty Race! You can accomplish what you will!"), frightened both whites and more mainstream black-rights agencies, and thus the U.S. government used its newly formed Federal Bureau of Investigation to dismantle and discredit the organization. Garvey was jailed and, in 1927, deported back to Jamaica. And in the mid-1920s, the Ku Klux Klan, riding a wave of white push-back against the advances made by African Americans, gained huge political power. In 1925 they staged a

---

[3] Langston Hughes, "The Negro Artist and the Racial Mountain." The Nation (June 23, 1926). Available at: www.hartford-hwp.com/archives/45a/360.html.

massive march on Washington DC (the largest up until Martin Luther King Jr's march in 1963), and throughout the 1920s came to control the legislatures of six states while open members of the KKK were elected to both the U.S. House and Senate. In Doris Harper Allen's home state of Virginia, Harry F. Byrd, an avowed racist and die-hard supporter of segregation, became governor in 1926 and then later one of its Senators—a role he held until 1965 and from which he launched Virginia's "Massive Resistance" movement against the desegregation mandated by the Supreme Court's *Brown v. Topeka Board of Education* ruling in 1954. Doris Harper Allen's life thus began at a time of racial tension and reckoning—a time that continued to color her entire life.

    Doris Harper Allen's parents, Leo and Julia Harper, married in 1923 amidst this modernizing boom time, and by the time they welcomed Doris into the world, they did so from a house they had just finished building at 190 (later renumbered as 194) Effinger St. This property was in the midst of the African American community of Newtown that sat at the northeast edge of Harrisonburg. When Doris was born, Leo was working a variety of jobs, cleaning houses, tending gardens, and catering baked goods—work he initiated and managed himself as his own boss. Julia also worked as a cook and baker, often at the Normal School (that later became Madison College and then James Madison University), but increasingly she spent more time at home with what would eventually be their six children: Alfred (b. 1923), Carmelita (b. 1924), Julia (b. 1925), Doris (b. 1927), Leo Jr. (b. 1929), and Earnest (b. 1930).

    Times were always hard for black people in America's segregated society, but they got even harder when, just a month after Doris's second birthday, the New York Stock Market crashed launching what would become the decade-long Great Depression. In 1930, Harrisonburg was a solidly agricultural town of just 7,232 people, full of small businesses and industries that supported the wheat and dairy farms, poultry producers, and apple orchards that abounded in this area of the Shenandoah Valley. But though times were economically very trying during Doris Harper Allen's childhood, she had the advantage of being supported and nurtured by a strong and proud African American community that was then over three hundred years old.

From the time the English privateer ship, *White Lion*, brought captured Africans to Jamestown in 1619, Virginia has been a place defined and driven by questions of race. Though these first black people were not enslaved, within just a few decades the white officials of the area began to make enslavement the norm for non-white people in Virginia. These "founding families" of the state passed laws that stripped black and native people of all their rights and, by the end of the 1600s, the laws they created legally denied the humanity of all non-white residents, defining them as property not people. This is the foundational, evil reality of chattel slavery and the racism it came to create. These laws were firmly codified in the Virginia Slave Codes of 1705, and for the next century and a half the weight of these laws colored Virginia culture, mandating that over one third of Virginia's citizens were, paradoxically, not people. This evil paradox today seems almost incomprehensible as we wrestle with the reality that America's "Founding Fathers" such as George Washington, Thomas Jefferson, and James Madison—the men who led the fight against the oppression of rights by an unjust government and who penned the Declaration of Independence and the U.S. Constitution—were also all proud white Virginians who, combined, enslaved more than one thousand human beings, utterly denying their rights and humanity. This reality makes one question how "self-evident" these white Virginians really did find the truths that they so boldly proclaimed—"that all men are created equal, that they are endowed by their Creator with certain unalienable Rights, that among these are Life, Liberty and the pursuit of Happiness."

But though the laws of Virginia and the United States Constitution itself legally sanctioned and even encouraged their oppression, black and native peoples continued to find ways to assert their humanity and dignity. In thousands of small, everyday ways they pushed back, preserving their culture and constructing new identities, traditions, and institutions in the margins of society they controlled. Well-planned resistance was common, forcing white Virginians to maintain slave-patrols and armed forces to "keep the peace," but even so, Gabriel Prosser's planned rebellion in Richmond in 1800, and Nat Turner's violent revolt in 1831 in Southampton County showed that Virginia's black population had no intention of remaining enslaved. The economic realities of Virginia also created some unique situations. By the mid-1700s Tobacco production, the state's major agricultural export and the driver of its economy, slumped due to overproduction, and thus the need for enslaved labor decreased. Because of that, Virginia's free-black population did begin to increase, expanding from just 1.7% of the state's total population in 1790, to 3.7% by 1820. However, during that same period, the total enslaved population still increased, hitting 40.3% of the total population in 1810. The horrid reality was that enslaved humans themselves became one of Virginia's largest "products." In 1808 the United States banned the importation of enslaved people, and this caused a shortage of available labor just as a new cash crop, cotton, was beginning to boom in the states further to the south and west. This economic reality became an ethically horrifying economic opportunity for Virginia's slave owners as they began to purposefully and often forcefully ensure that their enslaved women produced as many children as possible—a new "crop" that they sold for their own profit.[4]

In the Shenandoah Valley of Virginia, and especially in Rockingham County, slavery was also very much a horrid reality, but it operated a bit differently. Nestled between the Blueridge and Allegheny Mountains and with the north and south forks of the Shenandoah River running through it, this fertile valley became the bread-basket of the region, producing huge amounts of wheat and corn in its fields and apples in its orchards, products that could be shipped by river to the more populated areas of Richmond to the south or Washington DC and Baltimore to the north. And

---

[4] See Ned Sublette & Constance Sublette, *The American Slave Coast: A History of the Slave-Breeding Industry* (Chicago Review Press, 2015).

these crops were less labor-intensive than products such as tobacco, cotton, and rice, thus less enslaved labor was needed in the region. Furthermore, beginning in the mid-1700s, this fertile farm land was largely settled by Mennonites and Brethren, pacifist religious groups that forbade their members from owning slaves, not because they were less racist or more tolerant than their fellow white neighbors, but because slavery necessitated violence which their faith forbade. Thus, compared to the Virginia-wide average of nearly a 40% enslaved population, in rural Rockingham County, those numbers were far less. The 1810 census shows 11.7% of the total population enslaved and 1.7% free people of color, and in 1840 11.4% were enslaved and 2.7% were free. And the majority of the county's free black population lived in the biggest town of the area, Harrisonburg—the eventual home of Doris Harper Allen and the community of Newtown.[5]

In the decades before the Civil War and the passing of the 13th Amendment that ended slavery, a small but vibrant community of free blacks already called Harrisonburg home. In 1810 the census records thirteen heads of household in Rockingham County as "FN" (Free Negro) and a total of 213 individuals marked as "free persons" who are not white and not "Indians." In the 1820 census they recorded Harrisonburg separately from the county; this shows that of the 257 free blacks living in the county as a whole, there were thirteen families headed by free blacks living in Harrisonburg, and that six of them were engaged in "commerce," meaning they were running businesses of their own. The 1850 census (the first that included the names and ages of all family members) shows eighty-one free black individuals living in Harrisonburg. Fifteen of them were living with white families, usually as live-in help, but the remaining sixty-six resided in black-headed households that were often also successful family businesses. For example, 56-year-old Jeremiah Gibson and his wife Peggy lived with their two adult sons John

---

[5] This data comes from the census records and slave registries of Rockingham County and Harrisonburg Virginia (1790–1860), made available via familysearch.org. Thanks to Isaac Sawin who helped compile this information.

and St. Clair who, with their father, were wagon-makers. Samuel Hite was a successful blacksmith who headed a household of five other free-blacks, including two young apprentices, Joseph Gasnor (16) and Samuel Hyke (13). John Jones and his wife Maria supported a family of six as cake bakers; Maddison Mahoe headed a family of five as a well-digger, and he seems to have worked with William Strother, another well-digger who, along with his wife Mary, cared for a family of nine. Most successful of these free black families were the Peters. Joshua Peters shows up as a free black man already in the 1810 census as a successful saddle and harness maker. By 1850 he had passed away, but his sons, William (30) and James (22) were continuing the successful business and supporting large families. According to the writings of Marla Graham Koontz Carr, a white citizen of Harrisonburg born in 1812, the Peters were well-respected in town as master craftsmen. She noted that their "work was made of the best material, in the finest style," and that they employed many people, including "several white men," at their thriving business on Market Street.[6]

But just to keep this in context, these free-black success stories, while important and certainly worth celebrating, were also very much the exception. These few free black families lived in a society that assumed that people who looked like them were, by definition, slaves. By the 1850s, Virginia had laws firmly in place that made it illegal to teach black people to read or write; and other laws that required any newly-freed black people to leave the state within a year or risk being re-enslaved. Harrisonburg's free black residents were eighty-one people living in a county that held 2,267 of their brothers and sisters in bondage. In a telling example of the dehumanizing nature of this reality, though the 1850 census recorded the names of each of their masters, these thousands of enslaved people were only recorded by their gender, age, and color (black or "mulatto")—their names went unrecorded. And these indignities were getting worse, not better, during the 1850s.

---

[6] See 1810, 1820, and 1850 U.S. Census data for Rockingham County, VA; and, John Walter Wayland, *Historic Harrisonburg* (C. J. Carrier & Co.: 1949), 55.

The Compromise of 1850 laid out by Congress to help resolve tensions between Northern and Southern states that erupted over debates about the new territories captured during the Mexican American War, included the Fugitive Slave Act that made it a crime to assist a person of color trying to escape the bonds of slavery. And even more egregiously, the 1857 *Dred Scott* decision by the Supreme Court spelled out two terrible new realities for non-white people. First, it stated that the Constitution protected individual property in all states, thus making it illegal for any state to ban slavery because enslaved people were not legally people but property—their owners thus had the right to take them wherever they wanted. Second, and even more horrifically, Chief Justice Roger Taney, writing for the 7-2 majority, ruled that the founders never intended to extend rights to non-white people and thus they "are not included, and were not intended to be included, under the word 'citizens' in the Constitution, and can therefore claim none of the rights and privileges which that instrument provides for and secures to citizens of the United States."

Further, he wrote that a "perpetual and impassable barrier was intended to be erected between the white race and the one which they had reduced to slavery."[7] In other words, according to this new ruling, the United States of America, beginning with its founding documents and extending out to all its state and local laws, was a country that guaranteed life, liberty, and the pursuit of happiness to white people only. Black people, whether enslaved or free, had no rights in the United States. This was a profound legal change. Though the U.S. Constitution did not forbid slavery, and infamously also proclaimed that enslaved black people should be tallied as just 3/5 of a person in census counts, many of the founders had, at least philosophically, opposed slavery. Indeed Madison and Jefferson, though themselves large slave owners, saw the institution of slavery as wrong—a "necessary evil" that they hoped would come to an end. But by the mid-1800s, this was no longer the case. Influential South Carolina senator and former vice-president John C. Calhoun proclaimed in the 1840s that

---

[7] See *The Dred Scott Decision: Opinion of Chief Justice Taney*. Available at: www.loc.gov/resource/llst.022/?st=gallery.

slavery was not a "necessary evil" but a "positive good." The new laws and rulings of the 1850s built upon that sentiment. More than ever before in United States history, statements of white superiority and black inferiority were being codified into law. For black Americans, things were not getting better; they were getting much, much worse.

Chief Justice Taney and most of the legislators of the Southern slave states hoped that these strict new mandates would settle the "slavery question" once and for all—that the United States would always be a land of free whites and enslaved blacks. But that is not what happened. Four years after the *Dred Scott* ruling, tensions over the question of slavery intensified to the point that the nation erupted into civil war when the slave-holding states removed themselves from the United States to form a new nation: The Confederate States of America. This new nation's founding documents borrowed most of their language from the United States' Constitution, but they added one obvious and important addition—the guarantee of race-based slavery forever, and the explicit statement that citizenship and rights were granted only to white people. The only role for blacks within this new nation was enslavement. As tensions rose to the point of war, Alexander Stephens, the Vice President of the new Confederate States of America, gave a speech in which he explained the Confederacy's new government. He proudly proclaimed that, "its foundations are laid, its corner-stone rests, upon the great truth that the negro is not equal to the white man; that slavery and subordination to the superior race is his natural and normal condition." And he emphatically concluded, "This, our new government, is the first, in the history of the world, based upon this great physical, philosophical, and moral truth."[8]

But despite the Confederacy's confident statements of white superiority, statements that many Northern whites believed as well, the nations' 4.4 million black residents, as well as many of its white citizens, did not believe this lie. Refusing to recognize the

---

[8] See Alexander Stephens, "Cornerstone Speech" (March 21, 1861). Available at: http://teachingamericanhistory.org/library/document/cornerstone-speech/.

Southern states' rights to leave the union (an idea that led to later justifications that the Civil War was about "States Rights") the new president, Abraham Lincoln, mustered troops to forcibly maintain the union. Like their Southern brethren, Northern whites had also been raised with assumptions of white superiority, and initially the Union refused to recruit or use any black men to fight, fearing the idea of an empowered and armed black citizenry. But thanks to the efforts of black reformers and advocates such as Frederick Douglass, Harriet Tubman, and Sojourner Truth, who lobbied Lincoln to end slavery and allow black people to join the fight for their rights and humanity—a fight they had already been fighting on their own for over two centuries—Lincoln and his Republican colleagues came to support this idea. Though it was hugely controversial among many white Northerners, and though it didn't free enslaved people in states controlled by the Union, Lincoln issued the Emancipation Proclamation, officially freeing all enslaved people in the rebellious states as of January 1, 1863. Further, new federal law also granted black people the right to join the Union army—a right that thousands of black men quickly embraced. At the very minimum, 5,723 black men from Virginia mustered into the Union Army, and the total is likely more than double that number as many black Virginians had been sold off to other states before the war, or had fled to other territories during the war, and thus joined from those locations. Virginia mustered in multiple black fighting units for the Union forces, including the 2nd U.S. Colored Cavalry; the 2nd U.S. Colored Artillery; and the 2nd, 10th, 23rd, and 38th Colored Infantry units.[9]

The violence of the Civil War was powerfully felt in Harrisonburg because the Shenandoah Valley stood between the Union capital of Washington DC and the Confederate capital of Richmond, Virginia, and thus battles erupted throughout the region, resulting ultimately in the burning of the valley by Union forces in 1864. Virginia as a state had been hesitant to join the Confederacy—it did not initially split away, and it was only after

---

[9] See "United States Colored Troops" in the *Encyclopedia of Virginia*. Available at: encyclopediavirginia.org/entries/united-states-colored-troops-the/.

four contentious rounds of voting that it ultimately did join the Confederate cause. And much of the state ultimately did not leave—the western counties stayed loyal to the Union and amidst the heat of the war split from Virginia to form the new pro-Union state of West Virginia in 1863. Rockingham County was on the very edge of this split—the counties just beyond it joined West Virginia—but it remained in Virginia despite the fact that many of its citizens, especially the Mennonites and Brethren, strongly opposed joining the Confederate cause.

This is an important part of history that is often ignored—support of secession and slavery was not a clear North and South issue among the nation's white citizens. There were many white Northerners who opposed the end of slavery and supported the Confederacy, especially in the Mid-West, and there were many white Southerners who fought against the Confederacy. For example, though Virginians Robert E. Lee and Thomas "Stonewall" Jackson famously went on to lead the military efforts of the Confederacy in Virginia, forty percent of Virginia's officers actually stayed loyal to Lincoln and fought for the Union, and across the South, in every state but South Carolina, white men left their home communities to join the Union effort against the Confederacy—in total, over 100,000 of them. But while slavery and the Confederacy may have been a contentious issue among whites in the nation, it was not among the black population. Despite claims to the contrary, there was never any organized black support of the Confederacy—black people universally joined the Union cause and fought valiantly and bravely to gain their freedom. Ultimately, 180,000 African Americans signed up to fight for their freedom, making up one tenth of the total Union army. These men paid a heavy price—approximately one third of them died fighting for the freedom of their people.[10]

---

[10] See John L. Heatwole, "The Burning: The Fire and Sword of War" (2015). Available at: www.shenandoahatwar.org/the-burning-the-fire-and-sword-of-war/; James Alex Baggett, *The Scalawags: Southern Dissenters in the Civil War and Reconstruction* (Louisiana State University Press, 2003); Sam Smith, "Black Confederates: Truth and Legend."

In the years immediately following the Civil War, African Americans continued to fight hard, striving to force the United States to recognize their hard-won gains and to ensure that they would never again be treated as second-class citizens. Legally, they won these battles, as the U.S. Constitution came to include the 13th amendment (1865) that ended slavery; the 14th amendment (1868) guaranteeing citizenship to all people born in or naturalized into the United States; and the 15th amendment (1870) that guaranteed that, "The right of citizens of the United States to vote shall not be denied or abridged by the United States or by any State on account of race, color, or previous condition of servitude." Between 1868 and 1877 black people across the nation embraced their power to vote and put more than 1,500 black men into state and national legislative offices, including two U.S. Senators and fourteen U.S. House members. And even after Reconstruction ended in 1877, black people continued to hold tenaciously onto their rights even amidst growing opposition, electing hundreds more black people into office and winning black members seats in the U.S. House fourteen more times before 1900.[11]

Perhaps even more importantly, black families across the nation worked incredibly hard to climb out of the absolute poverty they began with, for though they were freed, most were given no material resources to compensate them for the years of tortuous labor they had endured. They were thus largely on their own to gain and property and to reunite and establish families, communities, and organizations that they themselves could control. The short-lived U.S. Freedmen's Bureau (1865–1872) provided some assistance in the form of legal representation,

---

Available at: www.battlefields.org/ learn/articles/black-confederates-truth-and-legend; and, Library of Congress, "African American Soldiers during the Civil War." Available at: www.loc.gov/classroom-materials/united-states-history-primary-source-timeline/civil-war-and-reconstruction-1861-1877/african-american-soldiers-during-the-civil-war/.

[11] See United States House of Representatives, "Black-American Members by Congress, 1870-present." Available at: history.house.gov/Exhibitions-and-Publications/BAIC/Historical-Data/Black-American-Representatives-and-Senators-by-Congress/.

education, and aid in locating family members, but it was poorly funded and often served as a mechanism that hurt more than helped, for while it did do good work helping to establish black schools, it often also forced black workers into exploitative sharecropping contracts with white land owners.

Just as it had been slow in joining the Confederacy, Virginia was also slow in rejoining the Union—a process that wasn't completed until 1870, several years after most Southern states had already rejoined. In the years between 1870 and 1900, eighty-five black members were elected to the Virginia Congress and one to the U.S. Congress from Virginia, John Mercer Langston, though his win was contested and he was ultimately only able to serve a few months of his term. Such pushback against black rights sadly became the norm in Virginia and across the nation in the years leading up to 1900, as rights were again systematically stripped away via unjust "Jim Crow" laws that restricted African American voting despite the guarantees of the 15th amendment. It is telling that in Virginia, the resistance that kept John Mercer Langston from rightfully filling his seat in Congress after the 1890 election, only hardened after he arrived in Washington. He was soundly defeated in the next election as black voters were increasingly disenfranchised, and it would be over one hundred years before Virginia would again elect a black person to serve in the U.S. Congress—African American Robert C. Scott finally won a seat again in 1993.[12]

In Harrisonburg and Rockingham County, the black population was always less than fifteen percent of the total population and thus never able to elect one of its own into public office during the years after the Civil War. But despite this, they made significant gains in many other ways. Already in 1868, the Freedmen's Bureau brought three Northern women into the area to help launch classes for the black population. In 1869 William and Hannah Carpenter deeded a parcel of land just outside of Harrisonburg for the settlement of recently-freed black families,

---

[12] Ibid; and *Encyclopedia Virginia*, "African American Legislators in Virginia, 1867-1899." Available at: encyclopediavirginia.org/entries/african-american-legislators-in-virginia-1867-1899/.

and this area became the community of Athens, later renamed Zenda, which included Long's Chapel, a one-room building that served as both a church and school by 1870.

This era in Harrisonburg's African American history is especially marked by the life of Lucy Simms, a woman who was born in 1856 as an enslaved member of the Gray family of Harrisonburg. She had been named for her grandmother whom the Gray family had purchased from one of Abraham Lincoln's slave-holding cousins (also named Abraham Lincoln) who lived just outside of Harrisonburg, and when freedom came at the end of the Civil War, Lucy immediately sought an education. Gaining the basic skills she needed from the Freedmen's Bureau's classes and then from the new state-sponsored schools established by Virginia when it rejoined the Union in 1870, by 1874 she qualified to enroll at Hampton Institute, a school established to provide higher education for the recently freed black population. At Hampton she was a classmate of famed African American leader and eventual founder and president of Tuskegee Institute, Booker T. Washington. By 1877 she came back to the Harrisonburg area, teaching first at Zenda, and then in Harrisonburg starting in 1878. In 1882, funds were raised by the local black community to supplement the funds provided by the local school board to build the Effinger Street School which opened in 1883. This is the school that sat across the street from Doris Harper Allen's house and where she went to school, studying under Ms. Lucy Simms in 1934 at the very end of Simms' 56-year teaching career—by that time she had taught three generations of many of Newtown's families.[13]

---

[13] See Nancy Bondurant Jones, *An African American Community of Hope: Zenda, 1869–1930* (Long's Chapel Preservation Society, 2007); and James Madison University, the Shenandoah Valley Black Heritage Project, and the "Celebrating Simms Exhibit." Available at: https://omeka.lib.jmu.edu/simms/exhibits/. For a full telling of the life of Lucy Simms, see Dale MacAllister's, *Lucy Frances Simms: From Slavery to Revered Public Service* (Staunton, VA: Lot's Wife Press, 2020).

The area that became Doris Harper Allen's beloved "Newtown"—a name often given to areas where formerly-enslaved people settled—began to form at the northeastern edge of Harrisonburg shortly after the war. In her well-researched book on her ancestors who helped establish the Newtown community, *Keeping Up With Yesterday* (2009), Ruth M. Toliver notes that her great-grandfather, Ambrose Dallard, and his twin brother Reuben, along with William Johnson, had all been enslaved by the Yancey family who owned the "Riverbank" estate near Elkton, Virginia, about fifteen miles southeast of Harrisonburg. After the war, these three men moved to Harrisonburg and began working at the Houck Tannery. It was hard, undesirable work, but it paid well. By 1869 they used their earnings to buy multiple building plots, and with lots of ingenuity, thrift, and hard work, began building the homes, churches, and schools that became Newtown. And they were not alone in these efforts. By 1870 black residents Jane Anderson, John Cooper, Franklin Lewis, Annie Byrd, Thomas and Melinda Givens, and Albert, H. W. and Walter Francis, along with Ambrose and Reuben Dallard and William Johnson, had all purchased property in "Zirkles Addition" which came to be known as Newtown. Situated just five blocks northeast of downtown Harrisonburg on land between the "Hill Top Farm" and "Collicello," mansions owned by the Gray family, one of the largest slaveholding families in the Valley, this resilient community created its own world. Though its residents worked in the stores and restaurants and produced many of the goods that drove Harrisonburg's economy, Jim Crow laws barred them from these same establishments and thus in Newtown they created their own shops, churches, and places of recreation—their own small town inside the larger city of Harrisonburg. (see map opposite).[14]

---

[14] See chapter two, "Pioneers, Oh Pioneers" in Ruth M. Toliver, *Keeping Up With Yesterday* (Self-Published, 2009), 19-39.

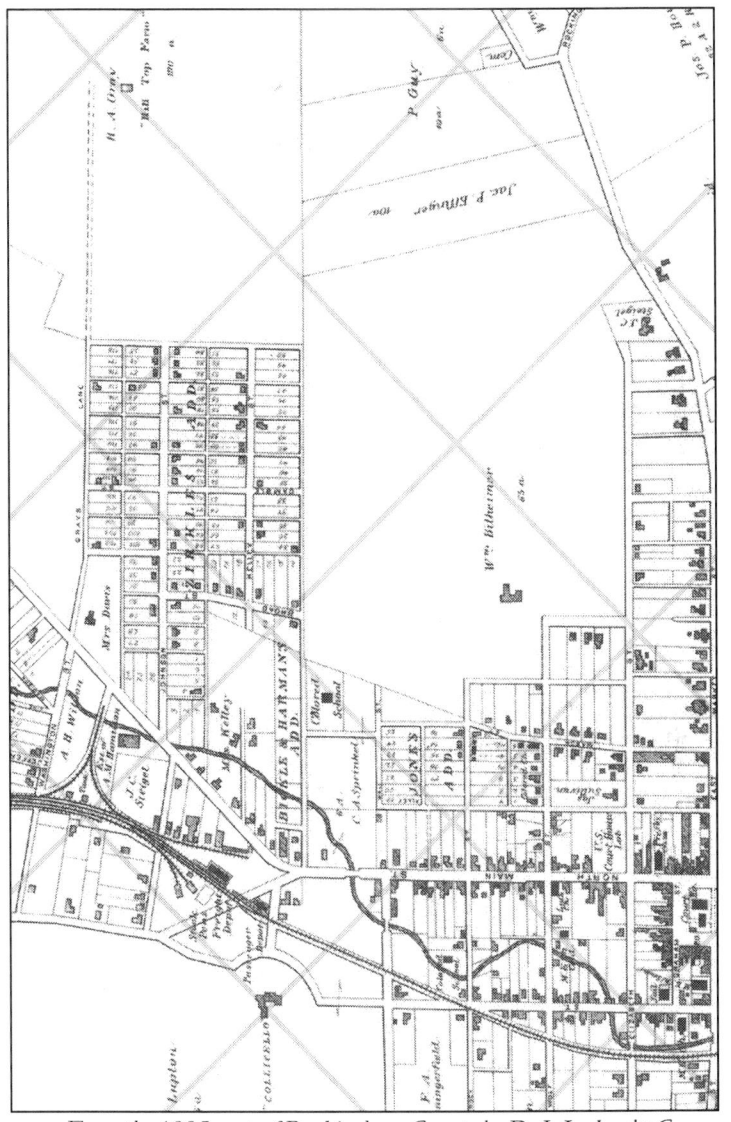

*From the 1885 map of Rockingham County by D. J. Lake & Co.
Available at: www.historicmapworks.com/Atlas/US/11069/.*

Doris Harper Allen's grandparents were among the early residents of Newtown, and by the time of Doris's birth in 1927, it was a community filled with her family. Her paternal grandfather, John Howard (c.1856–1920) was likely born into slavery as his parents, Jacob (b. 1836) and Sophia Moten Howard (b. 1837) don't show up in any census records before the 1870s, suggesting they were enslaved. In 1882 at the age of twenty-six, John Howard married sixteen-year-old Cordelia Davis (1866–1941)—she was of Native American as well as African American decent and spoke the Catawba language. Their first child, Earnest, was born in 1884, followed by Lucy (1888), Mary (1890), then Bessie in January and Cuetta in December of 1896, and finally Leo (Doris's father) in 1901. The pressure to earn a good living kept John away from the house during many of the family's early years—the 1900 and 1910 census show him working away from home and Cordelia and the kids living in a rented house on Johnson Street where Cordelia worked as a seamstress to help make ends meet. But despite the distance, the family unit was tightknit and soon prospered. All the kids went to the Effinger Street School just a few blocks away, and by the 1910s, John became a foreman at a local dye works and he and Cordelia were able to buy several lots and to build their own home at 188 Effinger Street, just across from the school. They lived there together until his death in 1920 and she remained there for another twenty years thereafter.

Doris Harper Allen's mother, Julia Hughes Howard (1905–1994), was also born and raised in Harrisonburg. Her father, Hezekiah Hughes, was born enslaved in York County, Virginia in 1859. In 1865 the Freedman's Bureau recorded him as working as a six-year-old, noting that he "culls oysters." It seems that he and his family then moved to Rockbridge County, and there his sisters, Mary Banks and Annie Stewart, settled, married, and raised families. By 1900 Hezekiah had moved to Harrisonburg and married a woman named Anna; they had two children, Minnie (b. May 1893), and Fannie (b. Sept. 1894). In late-1900, Anna died and Hezekiah married Willanna Montgomery (b. 1876) shortly thereafter. The 1910 census shows they had another three children, William (b. 1901), Arlene (b. 1902), and finally Julia F.

(Doris's mother) in 1905. Hezekiah's mother, Tishia J. Hughes lived with them in their rented house near the passenger railroad station on West Market Street until she passed away in July of 1907. By 1910, Minnie was seventeen and still living with them and, along with Willanna, was working as a servant for white families while Hezekiah worked doing odd jobs. Ten-year-old William worked as a delivery boy for a local dairy while also attending the Effinger School with Arlene and tending to four-year-old Julia.[15]

So it was that in the early 1910s, both the Howard and the Hughes children were attending the Effinger School, studying under the watchful eye of Lucy Simms and a cadre of other dedicated African American teachers. Though their school was far from "equal" in terms of resources to their white counterparts—the state provided them far less money and no transportation for black schools—the students of the Effinger Street School gained strong educations. Indeed, in the early years of Virginia public schools (which first began for both whites and blacks in 1870—Virginia hadn't had public education before the Civil War) the black teachers were often better-educated than many of their white counterparts thanks to the efforts of schools like Hampton Institute. Having been denied an education for so long, black families eagerly pushed their children to succeed, and the Howard and Hughes families were no exception. For example, a 1915 newspaper account shows that ten-year-old Julia Hughes was a finalist in a declamation contest.[16] Both she and Leo Howard took classes through the seventh-grade level (the common stopping point for most children, black and white, in this era) while also focusing on building skills and trades. Both of them became

---

[15] Information about Hezekiah Hughes and Willanna Montgomery is scant. Willanna shows up as Hezekiah's wife in the 1910 Census for Harrisonburg, and the Virginia Register of Births shows her born in April of 1876 in the Grants River district of Rockbridge County, VA, the same place Hezekiah's sisters lived. Her parents were Washington and Edmonia Lee Montgomery.

[16] See "Declamation Contest Among Colored Pupils," *Daily News-Record* (Harrisonburg, Feb. 16, 1915), 17.

excellent cooks, bakers, gardeners, and cleaners. They married on June 4, 1923 and began a cleaning business that Leo ran for the rest of his career while Julia worked as a cook at Madison College. Children soon followed: Alfred Lee born in 1923, Carmelita Frances (1924), Julia Lorraine (1925), Doris Jean (1927), Leo Jr. (1929), and Earnest (1930).

As Doris Harper Allen's memoir here abundantly shows, by the time she was born in 1927, she was surrounded by a large family that was firmly integrated into the Newtown community. Her parents had the funds to own their own home by the mid-1920s and they built at 190 Effinger Street, right next door to Leo's parent's house, where, by the mid-1920s, his mother Cordelia lived with his sister Cuetta and her three children. On the other side of her house was more family—Leo's other sister Bessie married Thomas "Frank" Mosby, a laundryman, in 1916, and they raised their eight children at 186 Effinger. And just a few more houses down, at 134 Effinger, lived Leo's oldest brother Earnest and his two sons. Though Julia's parents did not stay in Harrisonburg, other family did—her half-sister Minnie married Henry Stuart, the head cook at Harrisonburg's prestigious Kavanaugh Hotel, and they owned their own two-story house just a few blocks away at 629 North Broad Street where they raised their children. Doris Harper Allen thus grew up surrounded by multiple aunts and uncles and no less than fifteen cousins, all relatively close to the same age. And though she rightly notes in her memoir that they were "poor but didn't know it," it is also abundantly clear that her family was part of a striving and advancing black middle-class—people who ran their own businesses, stressed education to their children, actively participated in church and civic organizations, and built their own solidly middle-class homes, complete with phones and other modern conveniences many white folks didn't yet have. They are a keen example of the "American Dream"—people who in two generations went from slavery to the middle-class.

This striving for success is important to note, because unlike the rags to riches stories often told and celebrated among white Americans, the stories Doris Harper Allen tells here demonstrate the added challenges faced by equally ambitious black Americans who had to contend with the daily injustices of Jim Crow America. Newtown residents were entrepreneurial because they were driven by ideas of success, but also because they were barred from most of the routes toward success that were open to white Americans. Doris met her first husband, Robert Lee Harper, when she worked delivering food for his parent's business, Bill and Della's Chicken Box, which they ran out of the back of their home. Her future father-in-law, William Harper, was the chef at the Spotswood Country Club—a place he himself was never allowed to join or dine. Her future mother-in-law, Della Harper, was the chief cook at a local hotel where she wasn't allowed to stay. And Doris was working for them because after graduating from Simms, going to a local college wasn't an option and so she delivered food while also cooking for the president of Madison College—one of the few roles open to her in that institution of higher learning during the Jim Crow era.

Throughout this memoir, Doris Harper Allen shows both the harsh realities and the humane kindnesses that marked her years in Newtown. By the time she left for Huntington, WV in 1970 after marrying her second husband, Hezekiah Allen, a lifetime postal worker who was well-connected to his activist-oriented black community, she had seen huge changes in her Newtown community. These included some good changes. The Civil Rights Movement began to make a real impact in the mid-1950s, and by 1963 she took her eldest son Robert to see Martin Luther King Jr. speak at the March on Washington. And though Virginia's "massive resistance" policies delayed school desegregation for more than a decade, her children—the "Three Bs": Belinda (b. 1950); Robert "Bob" (b. 1951); and William "Billo" (b. 1853)— wound up spending their last years of high school in integrated schools. They also grew up witnessing a mother who both talked the talk and walked the walk of creating change in the world.

As a young mother, Doris Harper lived the change she wanted to see. Though she had three kids under the age of three in the early 1950s, she remained active in local organizations— articles in Harrisonburg's *Daily News Record* show that she was both chairman and secretary of the African-American "Ladies Community Club" that organized many civic events, and by the mid-1950s, as her children entered school, she helped lead the Simms PTA, organizing the annual homecoming event that brought alumni flocking back to Newtown each summer. And she was active not just in the planning, she also participated—she was homecoming queen runner-up in 1955, and in 1958 her 14-point performance helped propel the alumni women's basketball team to a victory over the current high-school team![17]

Doris Harper on the right as runner-up in the Simms Homecoming Queen contest. Daily News Record *(July 6, 1955), p. 4.*

---

[17] See Harrisonburg *Daily News Record*: April 5, 1954, p. 3; Nov. 1, 1954, p. 3; June 6, 1955, p. 10; July 6, 1955, p. 4; Dec. 12, 1955, p. 15; Feb. 8, 1956, p. 23; and, March 18, 1958, p. 17.

Far more importantly, however, in the years after the *Brown v. Topeka Board of Education* ruling that was to have ended segregated schools, Virginia's "massive resistance" movement continued to prevent integration. Indeed in 1956, two years after *Brown*, Rockingham County built a new, white-only high school that was conspicuously named for the Confederate general Turner Ashby. By 1962, a "Citizens Committee" made up of black and white residents, formed to finally force Harrisonburg schools to desegregate. Though she was then a single-mother[18] working multiple jobs to support her family, Doris Harper threw herself into this cause, serving as the Northeast neighborhood's representative to the group. She also became even more civically active, working with the Federated Junior Girls, the Order of the Eastern Star, and as an elected member to the Executive Board of the Rockingham Council on Human Relations where she promoted full equity in all public recreation programs.[19]

Harrisonburg's Black Masonic Lodge's Order of the Eastern Star, 1963. Doris Harper is in the back row on the left.

---

[18] Doris Harper and Robert Lee Harper divorced in 1960.
[19] See Harrisonburg *Daily News Record*: April 23, 1962, p. 2; April 25, 1962, p. 1; Jan. 21, 1963, p. 10; July 22, 1966, p. 7, and March 17, 1970, p. 8.

But as she pushed so hard for change, Doris Harper came to see that "progress" was often executed in ways that continued to promote inequality. Like many other cities across the nation, in the late-1950s Harrisonburg took federal money to launch "Urban Renewal" projects. The Harrisonburg Redevelopment and Housing Authority then put plans R-4 and R-16 into effect in the early-1960s, removing some truly dilapidated housing (largely owned by absentee white landlords), but also destroying 60% of the black-owned homes and almost all of the black-owned businesses of Newtown.[20] Members of Doris Harper's family, like those of most other Newtown families, watched helplessly as their well-kept houses were claimed and razed via immanent domain rulings. At nearly this same time, desegregation finally came to the city schools, but Harrisonburg implemented it in ways that hurt the black community. They shuttered the Lucy Simms School—a fine, modern building in the heart of Newtown that had just been remodeled in 1961—and then bussed all of the black students across town to formerly white-only schools. This one-two punch of the destruction of the neighborhood by Urban Renewal and the shutting of the school that was at the heart of the Newtown community, radically altered the integrity and cohesion of Doris Harper's childhood home. This largely explains the title of her first memoir, *The Way It Was, Not The Way It Is*.

In 1970 Doris Harper remarried, joining with Hezekiah Allen to become Doris Harper Allen. She moved with him back to his home community in Huntington, West Virginia and quickly became deeply involved with the organizing efforts that he had promoted throughout his life. Though he died shortly thereafter, over the next thirty years, she threw herself into that work, serving on multiple boards and advocating tirelessly for marginalized people—she helped feed the homeless, she took in international

---

[20]See Randi B. Hagi, "The Legacy of Harrisonburg's 'Urban Renewal'." WMRA (Feb. 11, 2020). Available at: www.wmra.org/post/legacy-harrisonburgs-urban-renewal#stream/0. Extensive collections and documentation of these projects are available in the Robert James Sullivan Jr. Papers housed in James Madison University's special collections. Available at: https://commons.lib.jmu.edu/rjs/.

students, and she served HIV-positive people in the early years of the AIDS epidemic when few others would.

Though Urban Renewal and a clumsy desegregation process hurt Harrisonburg's black population, resilience is in the DNA of the Newtown community. By 2001 Doris Harper Allen refocused her attention back on her home community, moving back to Harrisonburg just as efforts were getting underway to remake and revitalize the community once again. In 2005, Newtown residents under the leadership of Karen Thomas created the Northeast Neighborhood Association (NENA), a group that helped launch many initiatives in the historically black section of town that included Newtown. The Lucy Simms School was repurposed as the Lucy F. Simms Educational Center which now houses multiple educational and civic programs and organizations. The Roberta Webb Daycare Center expanded its efforts to serve the area's children, and NENA bought the historic Dallard/Newman House in the heart of the community where it will function as a museum and library celebrating the neighborhood's history. In 2013 the Shenandoah Valley Black Heritage Project also launched in this neighborhood, largely driven by the efforts of Robin Lyttle who became a close friend of Doris Harper Allen. It, along with joint efforts with James Madison University, Eastern Mennonite University, and other local historians have produced a number of important projects on Urban Renewal, on the horrid spectacle of lynching that punctuated the very worst of Jim Crow's violent

Doris Harper married Hezekiah Allen on August 21, 1970

history in Virginia, and on the proud history and legacy of the Simms School and black education in Newtown.[21]

Doris Harper Allen's stories help weave together and illustrate this intricate and complex history, providing those of us trying to make sense of today with much-needed context and understanding. Doris Harper Allen has been celebrated and honored much these past few years, and for good cause, for though in many ways her stories are not extraordinary—they are much the same as the stories of struggle and resilience that are told by the many families who lived in Newtown—they are significant because she had the vision and drive to record them for posterity, ensuring that the story of her beloved community would be known for generations to come. It is indeed remarkable that now, as I type this introduction, Doris Harper Allen, though denied entrance into James Madison University because of Jim Crow, has been awarded its highest honor of a doctoral degree. Further, though she was banned from attending its classes and living on its grounds, now one of its prominent buildings bears her name. And though the laws and government agencies of her youth prevented her from shopping in Harrisonburg's stores or using it public facilities, her niece Deanna Reed is now its mayor. She recorded the stories of her community with the hope of bringing healing, justice, and equity through educating the next generation. Hopefully her words will help all of us move toward a new era of remembering, reckoning, repair, and re-creation. In that hope, I believe words from Doris Harper Allen's conclusion serve as the best way to end this introductory essay—"Education is and continues to make a difference in our society. We are not looking back, though we cannot help but think back. The march forward is greater for all people."

- Mark Metzler Sawin (January, 2023)

---

[21] See the webpages of the Northeast Neighborhood Association: www.nenava.org/; the Shenandoah Valley Black Heritage Project: valleyblackheritage.org/; and the "Celebrating Simms" project: omeka.lib.jmu.edu/simms/.

The Way It Was...

Coming of Age in Harrisonburg, Virginia in the Jim Crow Era

The Memoirs of Doris Harper Allen

Introduction

This is a story beginning more than eighty years ago. I was not born in slavery but felt enslaved during my childhood—"The Way it Was, not the Way it Is."[1] By this I mean you lived in poverty, you were poor and did not know it. I lived in a certain north section of town, in Harrisonburg, VA. You stayed in that section of town; you had three grocery stores run by local residents, three restaurants, a tea room, a barber shop, an ice cream parlor, a pool hall, a dance hall, five churches, and your own colored school. You stayed there: you had gardens to raise, livestock to take care of, and many children to raise in a peaceful, Christian neighborhood

---

[1] *The Way it Was, Not the Way it Is,* was the title of Doris Harper Allen's first book, published in 2015. The text presented here combines this book along with a later book she was working on at the time of her death and some of her other writings.

where everybody knew somebody. The 1930s, when I was young, was a long time ago, but even before then it was said that the "Old Master of the House" taught his servants how to do his rules, and his sayings ended up on the "Jim Crow" signs that we had to obey. There were those who were like servants with low self-esteem, born into illiterate families who could not read or write. According to the desires of the Old Master of the House, these servants were over-worked and mistreated. That was the Jim Crow of my childhood.

Born and raised in Harrisonburg, Virginia, for many years I played games of memory and pretending. I would daydream and meditate and make up stories to myself as though I was living somewhere else, and then I would go back and forth pretending it was true. I always imagined beautiful places and expensive surroundings, things I did not own and had only seen in a magazine or movie. It was fun. I did it often through my childhood. I would write notes of the beauty of mother nature, never completing them, put them in a book, and do some more later. I'd talk to myself about the weather or anything, make up stories about the animals and write them down. The mountains were my favorite, and I could go on and on about the Blue Ridge Mountains of Virginia. The Massanutten Mountains were also in my hometown. Then looking to the west of my Newtown section of the city are the Allegheny Mountains that look so near, but are far. I would drift off, get lost with thoughts of the surroundings; then I'd take out my book and scribble the beauty or daydream the imaginary. Often my pieces of paper didn't match, but I loved the feeling of satisfaction I would get just to release my emotion.

Where are all the bits of paper I started? I still have never collected or tried putting them together, but it seems not important. Now Father Time has put a hold on time—friends ask questions about the past, and I have answers. In panels open for discussion, I take part; when presentations are being made, I take part. My son kept bugging me: "Why don't you write a book? My friend at James Madison University said, "Why don't you write a book?" Finally I said to myself, "Can you? Will you?" "SURE," came a gentle word to me.

I began thinking about Martin Luther King Jr.'s visit to Washington, fifty years ago, when I and my twelve-year-old son went on the bus trip from Harrisonburg to Washington. Then I said to myself, "If you can think back fifty years, you can go beyond to eighty years." And it became fun and games all over again. So goes the story of how I began to write about the way it was, not the way it is. But beyond these remembrances, this is also a book about the shame and hurt persons of color endured. This is a witness to unkind expressions used a long time ago; an account of the true facts and sayings.

There is no place for Jim Crow today in our society. The evils of Jim Crow were disreputable and mean-spirited. If we open our hearts to love and charity, malice and hatred will no longer exist; they will fade away. We must ask…

> Create in me a clean heart, O God, and renew a right spirit within me. - Psalm 51:10

- Doris Harper Allen, 2019

Chapter I.
JIM CROW IN HARRISONBURG

The term "Jim Crow" originally referred to a black character in an old song, and was the name of a popular dance in the 1820s. Around 1828, the white performer Thomas "Daddy" Rice developed a routine in which he blacked his face, dressed in old clothes, and sang and danced in imitation of an old and decrepit black man. Rice published the words to the song, "Jump, Jim Crow," in 1830. The "Jump Jim Crow" song was popular and used excessively in downtown and other open areas of white entertainment. Colored people felt offended and tried hard to ignore the show.

Soon after, the term "Jim Crow Laws" began to be used to describe legislation passed during the Reconstruction era to restrict the rights of African-Americans—laws that became national with the Supreme Court's *Plessy v. Ferguson* ruling in 1896 that made "separate but equal" the law of the land. These laws continued as a means to justify segregation of the races through the 1960s.

When my son brought me the book called *The New Jim Crow* by Michelle Alexander; I told him she took my book title, *Jim Crow*, which is good.[23] She discusses the systematic incarceration of African American males and how it authorizes discrimination after their release. This shows that the discrimination and hardship of Jim Crow are still with us today.

---

[23] At the time of her writing this text, Doris Harper Allen was in the process of writing a book she had tentatively entitled, "Jim Crow in the 30s, 40s, 50s, and 60s: What Was Life Really Like Living Under Jim Crow Laws in Harrisonburg Virginia in the Shenandoah Valley?"

The Laws

The passage of the 13th and 14th amendments to the Constitution granted blacks the same legal protections as whites. However, after 1877, and the inauguration of Republican President Rutherford B. Hayes, Southern and border states began restricting the liberties of blacks.

Jim Crow then became the name of the racial caste system that operated primarily, but not exclusively, in Southern and border states between 1877 and the mid-1960s. Jim Crow was more than a series of rigid anti-black laws. It was a way of life. Under Jim Crow, African-Americans were relegated to the status of second-class citizens. Jim Crow both culturally and legally imposed racial inferiority. Though Jim Crow emerged as a minstrel character in the 1820s, it came to mean all the things that kept and portrayed African-Americans in an inferior status. Physical examples of this history are well documented at Ferris State University's Jim Crow Museum of Racist Memorabilia.[24]

In 1891, Homer Plessy, who was seven-eighths white and one-eighth black (therefore "black"), sat in the white-only Louisiana railroad coach reserved for whites and was arrested. Plessy was acting with a group of concerned citizens hoping to overturn the Jim Crow laws. They took the case to court, but the Louisiana courts ruled against Plessy. The case then went to the United States Supreme Court, which upheld the Louisiana court by a 7-1 vote, declaring that racial separation did not necessarily mean an abrogation of equality. Thus this "separate but equal" standard was established by the Supreme Court in *Plessy vs. Ferguson* (1896). Legally, Jim Crow was to create "separate but equal" treatment, but in practice Jim Crow laws condemned black citizens to inferior treatment and facilities.

African American leaders pushed back against Jim Crow strongly, and this was certainly true in Harrisonburg. As Ruth Toliver notes in her book about African American history in Harrisonburg, *Keeping Up with Yesterday* (2009), George A. Newman came to Harrisonburg in 1875 as principal of the 'colored school,'

---

[24]Ferris State University is in Big Rapids, Michigan. This exhibit can be seen virtually at https://www.ferris.edu/jimcrow/

and worked there in education for almost thirty years. G.A. Newman traveled as a deputy marshal for the federal government assigned to the Oklahoma Territory. That is the reason he was traveling on the railroad. Newman always traveled first class in his position as a deputy marshal until he boarded the train in Tennessee where he received the shock of his life at having to sit in the Jim Crow car. The poem he wrote expressed his outrage.

George A. Newman seated on left with family in 1903 or 1904 in Harrisonburg, VA. Image courtesy of Ruth Toliver.

The Jim Crow Car of Tennessee
By G. A. Newman, Harrisonburg, VA

Dear friends, I'm sorry to relate
It's known both near and far,
In Tennessee, that grand old State,
They use the Jim Crow Car;
And every colored citizen,
No matter what his fame,
Must ride inside that special den;
I tell you, it's a shame.

[Chorus]
*The Jim Crow Car of Tennessee
Is not the car for Me,
And if I only had a chance
I'd make the Legislature dance.*

The Jim Crow Car has seats for all
Who bear the fateful mark,
And, though you tower ever so tall
Get in: your skin is dark!
Your first-class fare is no defense,
Your ticket's but a lie;
A sham, an insult, a pretense;
This fact you'll not deny.

Chorus

We know not where to take our case
To get ourselves relieved.
As Uncle Sam's not in the race
When Africa's Sons are grieved;
So we must rise in self-defense.
Though humble we may be.
And show, by using common sense,
That we will still be free.

Chorus

No more excursions for our race
To this place and to that,
Let us presume it a disgrace,
And sit down on them flat.
Then when they see we have the grit
To boycott, near and far,
They'll change the law, and let us sit
In any proper car.

Final Chorus
The Jim Crow Car of Tennessee
Don't give us a fair show,
And, sure as Negros were made free,
The hateful Jim Crow Car Must Go.

Chapter 2
NEWTOWN NEIGHBORHOOD

Houses in Newtown in the 1930s. Most of these were destroyed during Harrisonburg's Urban Renewal projects of the early 1960s.

Newtown, a section in the northeast corner of Harrisonburg, was not a square or rectangle-shaped layout of streets. It was difficult for some to find their way, but not for those that lived there, including only a few whites who were compatible and easy to communicate with. They stayed on their turf as we called it. That was the way it was.

Newtown began on the corner of Johnson Street and Main Street, going east up to a path or lane on an unnamed street, which at present is named Simms Avenue, that runs north and south across Johnson Street to Kelley Street. Simms School had not been built. In fact, Washington Street, which runs parallel to Johnson Street, had not been extended to Vine Street from Main Street until 1934; after that the Simms School was built in 1938–39.[25]

---

[25] The Lucy F. Simms School was built in 1938–39 to replace the Effinger Street School which was condemned. Funding came from

Kelley's Field

The land which the school was built on was a big field which started at the corner of Washington and an unnamed lane and extended south going one block to Kelley Street. Kelley Street runs parallel to Johnson Street/Washington Street and was all in the Newtown area. Kelley Street became a dead end at the bottom of the hill, so we'd cross over Broad Street into Kelley's field owned by Mr. Kelley, a white gentleman who lived in a barn-red dwelling at the end of his property next to Blacks Run Creek that passed by, going further into the city.[26] Newtown bordered Kelley's Field on three sides. Main Street was central. Effinger Street, Johnson Street, and Broad Street were all around Kelley's Field.

Mr. Kelley spent most of his day on the porch with a loaded shot gun waiting for someone to cross his property. We took chances and played games with him all the time. He made it known he did not like certain races of people and used profanities to prove the law was on his side; the law said, "well, it was Mr. Kelley's property."

Kelley Street ran parallel to Effinger Street, Gay Street, Rock Street, Wolfe Street, all considered Newtown. Streets running parallel to Broad Street were Mason, Conrad, Federal Alley, also in Newtown. Effinger Street School was in the heart of Newtown and its grounds were available every day after 4 P.M. for citizens to pass through or play ball of any kind. The School was used only for the children under the supervision of the staff and opened by the janitor at 8:30 five days a week. Whenever the community used the School, it was under the direction of the School staff.

---

the Virginia Department of Education and the Works Project Administration. It served as the African-American school from 1939 until 1966 when desegregation came to Harrisonburg and the Simms School was shuttered and all black students sent to the formerly white-only public schools. Today the building functions as a community center run by the city of Harrisonburg.

[26] This was John E. Kelley; census data shows he was seventy-three in 1930 and living at 475 N. Main St. with his wife Ethel (56 years old) on a large property stretching up the hill beyond it, valued at $2,000.

A Garden of Plenty

Newtown had many vegetable gardens. Most families also raised chickens, had goats, cows, hogs, and a couple horses. In later years, those kinds of animals were banned in the city. There were lots of paths, fields, and hard surfaces, but no sidewalks. Wild flowers were plentiful, and street lights were very few. Newtown was country.

Just about every household had fruit trees. Some had one of each fruit. People canned, and children never went hungry unless someone said "no" and ran you off. Where Broad Street Mennonite Church stands on Broad Street today, was once an apple orchard plus one black heart cherry tree and two quince apple trees. We picked free apples and cherries all we wanted to. What we didn't eat went for pies and cooking at home. The orchard belonged to the property owners, and we were given permission to help ourselves.

In my yard, across the street from the church on Effinger, we had two mulberry, two pear, two cherry, a few quince, and two peach trees. Fruit was always welcomed at our house. What we did not eat was made into pies, stewed, fried, or canned. We walked two miles to Red Hill (now the area along Reservoir Street) to pick free as many as you wanted of blackberries, raspberries, and any other berry in the patch. We picked as many as we could because there was always ice cream to be made. The berries were free and in miles of open fields. We passed the little settlement of Red Hill, then a farm belonging to the Showker family. Their farm was larger than some we were used to seeing. The machinery was different from that of some farms, and there were more people working there. The animals (cows, sheep, horses, ducks, chickens, and more) were all moving like the story said 'Down on the Farm.' The hayloft was as large as the farm house. The rest was clear, wild, and open fields.

Household

We were poor and didn't know it. Everyone on Effinger Street and in Newtown burned kerosene or oil for lamps and wood or coal for cooking. Not any of us in the 1930–1940s had electricity, especially residents from Broad Street down Effinger Street where I lived. The row of twenty-seven homes after my residence were privately owned by investors, and their substandard houses did not meet standard code. There was improper wiring and plumbing throughout the dwellings. No storm windows, no furnaces or carpet on the bare wooden floors. Only linoleum covered the floors throughout the dwellings. There was no air conditioning, no driveways or garages. Cars, if any were owned, were parked on the street.

Kerosene lamps were used throughout the dwellings. Wood stove, coal, or oil were the heating methods. At that time coal was sold by the ton. If you had an outside building to put it in, which most people did not, you could store it there. Most of the coal was just put on the ground and stayed there as you used it throughout the winter. If ordered by the ton, coal was delivered. Otherwise, coal was purchased by the burlap sack full. You could purchase it loose for as much as 25¢ or 35¢ per sack. You hauled it on a wagon, you pulled it by hand, and some people carried the coal on their backs. From where we lived in Newtown it was thirteen blocks, so the wagon was fine with us, unless our parents had gotten a ton. At our house we had a cooking stove and a stove called the Heatrola, which burned coal. In winter, both stoves burned all night. Our parents took care of the stoves at all times. We children only emptied the ash pans.

Electricity was a long time being considered. When it did come in, it was tacky with wires that were run on the outside of the ceilings and woodwork. The plumbing was worse. Pipes ran also along the woodwork—because the houses had already been built, we could not tear into the walls. Again, we were happy and excited to have the conveniences. We did not complain about the unpleasant look of the situation.

No one had cement or grass around their house. They only had heavy wooden boards around to the back door. The "Board

Walk" around our house at 194 Effinger Street came to the back door for friends or family members. If you were special company or a bill collector, you came to the front door. Most front doors opened into the living room, and that room was neat at all times. The row of houses past my grandma's house were built high off the ground, and they had a cellar under the back end so there were stair steps at the back porch to go up on each of the twenty-seven units down Effinger Street, so the entrance to their homes had to be in the front.

Our house and grandma's house were built on the ground with cinder blocks for the foundation. From the side walk to our back door, we used six wooden doors (the knobs were already removed) placed flat on the ground, one after the other, straight to the back door. Dad would take our big play wagon and go to the junk yard, a mile away, get the wooden doors which cost 50¢ each, and haul them home, maybe making three trips. My brothers would go along to help. When we swept the front porch, we swept the Board Walk, we called it. When we scrubbed the front, we scrubbed the Board Walk around the house. We had an extra-large wagon and a few small ones. Wagons were a special at Christmas time for boys—no bicycle unless it was a three-wheeler. Scooters and wagons were popular.

Daddy laid a cement walk after I was in high school. The neighbors never got a walk, and later their houses were razed for the redevelopment of the city. We were poor and did not know it. We were constantly sweeping and mopping. Dad replaced the doors of the Board Walk when needed and replaced Grandma's boards around her house as well. You knew the Board Walk by heart. At night time it was dark. The only light would be coming from the living room window and the kitchen window. You got to the back door, and there was a lamp inside on the closed porch. We used kerosene lamps, and they gave out more light than you thought, maybe because you were used to them. Years later Dad wired our house, and we had electric lights all over. Mercy! Mercy!

The Newtown Community

People openly talked about Newtown like it was some city. You could hear one say, "I'm from Newtown."

"Where is that?"

"It's a section in the northeast of our city."

"Oh" would be the reply.

Our elders taught us Newtown is a good place to be. It was crime free, no robberies, no murders, safe for our children. We were proud people and respected our foreparents and children. This is true. I remember family at churches and school functions, their togetherness, how it spread throughout the community. Each family was happy and humble, with teachers and preachers in and out of our homes. We prayed together, we sang at all our gatherings, and we danced together and had happy days.

No break-ins, no vandalism, and lots of respect ran through the neighborhood during those days. Even after Effinger School closed in 1939, the building was used very little, but no one bothered it. The janitor lived across the street and kept his eye on the school. People got joy out of belonging to the neighborhood night watch (police walked a beat 24/7, they would say, even on Sundays). Children respected their elders and watched over them always with "yes ma'am" and "thank you." The northeast community joined together in the bitter or the sweetness of our lives. Newborn babies were always a joy, and childrearing was everyone's interest.

Every November, before Thanksgiving, as the weather was turning into our usual cold, frigid ice and snow, one-digit temperatures, it was time to butcher. My dad's friends would meet and help each other, one house at a time. During the butchering, children were taught to do chores. Mother had certain things to do, but she stayed busy and kept jobs going for everybody else. We liked the work because there was usually sing-a-longs, and everybody joined in.

Big, black, iron kettles were placed over chunks of red-hot burning wood, with boiling water for the hogs. After the hogs were killed, they were washed, then hung on scaffolds up high. It was so cold and most time a foot of snow on the ground; that way the meat could freeze overnight. Some meat was ground for sausage, some cut for hams—sugared cured or salted. Mercy, what a sight to see and remember! Cracklings being made, liver being cut, chitterlings being dumped! My mother and dad knew it all. We children helped and learned. The meat was kept in the smokehouse which was built in an area dug so many feet in the ground, oblong or square. Then a roof was put over it with siding like a house, and then a door. The smokehouse was cool in summer and very cold in winter; therefore, meat was kept well at a certain temperature.

In the 1930s, supermarkets were not around, and we dealt with our neighborhood grocery stores. Blacks and whites never socialized or communicated in public places, churches, or playgrounds, except for in grocery stores. Jim Crow laws did not play a part in the grocery stores.

Our grocery stores were owned by whites or colored. Coloreds and whites had no problem communicating there. The colored people ran charge accounts by the week, and at the end of each week you paid up your account and started again. Any and all were welcomed. The storeowner made the laws and rules which read "Welcome," and they personally knew all the customers. Families worked the store, either a husband and wife couple, or a family of husband, wife, and children.

Dixie Williams and his wife Mary, who were colored, had a big grocery store on Reservoir Street. Dixie raised his own chickens to sell, and sold fresh eggs from the chickens he raised. He raised all kinds of livestock and butchered in the fall every year. He cured his own hams. He was open from 7am until 11pm nightly. Mr. Dixie owned seven of the houses in the neighborhood. They did not have any children, but everyone loved them and treated them as if they were their parents.

Lloyd and Ethel Ball, colored, had a grocery store attached to the back of their home. They never had to go outside to enter their store. They lived on the corner of Mason and Elizabeth Streets and the store faced Mason.

Manners were a natural humble teaching of our families, our neighborhood, and our friends. We taught our children at home, at church, and gave privilege to the teachers at school to proceed. You never questioned them. We especially had to have good manners, sometimes referred to as table manners. Our children ask how we learned manners if they are not in the book. Manners are a practice of words that teach individuals right from wrong. Your elders used these words in everyday expressions and expected you to absorb them in your vocabulary and, in turn, use them where needed, like when someone gives you something, you say, "Thank you." If you do not want something given to you, you say, "No, thank you." When you answer elders, say "Yes sir" or "No sir." When you are offered an article, be polite and take one, not two or three.

Manners are a part of our character. They include kindness; as it is said, "to receive kindness, you must be kind." Manners include being polite and using the easy calm approach to others. Manners are a feeling of gratefulness you want to express to the other person for what they may have done. Manners includes prayer. We prayed together and alone, but there was always an expression of prayer. It is often said manners go a longways in helping us get a job or employment. One of the fruits of our foreparents' labors was good manners.

Chapter 3
FAMILY

Taken in 1930, 3-year-old Doris sits on the front porch of 194 Effinger Street, just across from what is now Broad Street Mennonite Church. [27]
Leo and Julia Howard built it in the late-1920s on property owned by Leo's parents. It was destroyed during Urban Renewal in 1962.

---

[27] Doris Harper Allen consistently remembered her address as 194 Effinger St., but census data from 1920, 1930, and 1940 all report Leo Howard's house as 190 Effinger St. It is possible that the numbering of the street shifted after 1940.

I was born in Rockingham County, the city of Harrisonburg, Virginia, on September 28, 1927, to Leo Howard and Julia Hughes Howard in their residence on East Effinger Street. I had three sisters and brothers before me and two after me. All six of us were born at home, delivered by a midwife. Our longevity has been in the high percent; one brother was killed in a car accident at age sixty, one brother is deceased at eighty-nine, a sister is deceased at eighty-nine, another sister is deceased at ninety. Our parents are deceased. Father died early at sixty-eight years and mother at the ripe old age of eighty-nine years.

My father's parents, John and Cordelia (Davis) Howard, lived next door to us. When the door swung open 24/7, we were always at the big house. Grandma Cordelia was light complexioned, and Grandpa John was African American.

Doris's Grandmother Cordelia Howard is seen here standing on her front porch at 188 Effinger Street. Doris's parents, Leo and Julia Howard, built their house next door in the late-1920s.

*Grandmother Cordelia Howard with Doris's siblings:
Julia, Carmelita, and Alfred Howard*

Grandma Cordelia was from Madison County, Virginia.[28] She was only four feet tall, part Native American and part African American. She was from the Catawba tribe, and she could speak the language of her people. (She never explained her English to us, maybe because we didn't ask, my sister said.) Though my grandmother was small in stature she was spicy in nature. She spoke softly, and she was quiet when rocking away in a rocking chair, while humming all day long. She would babysit with her grandchildren and never whipped anyone—she always showed us her stick yet never used it. She could cook and knew every weed that grew in her yard and garden. We didn't have things like spinach and kale. She'd just send us out to the garden to gather some "greens" and then she'd cook them. Weeds were used as medicine for cuts and burns, any ailments, vitamins—you holler and here comes the medicine man. There were no prescriptions—only Grandma's kitchen cabinet where all her medicine was kept.

Grandma Cordelia quietly taught us about the larger world. When public education for all children was initially forced upon the town by Federal law and the Virginia Constitution of 1868, Virginia's citizens supported separate schools for blacks and whites. Feelings ran so high that some invited the Ku Klux Klan, a vigilante group, to come to demonstrate its force to men and women of both races. They came in large numbers mounted (on horses) in their attire, headed by the New Market Brass Band, and paraded through town on New Years' Day, 1872. New Market is about 18 miles from Harrisonburg.

I learned from my grandmother and Aunt Minnie that a newspaper called *The Shenandoah Valley* in New Market, Virginia, published an article about the demonstration on January 4, 1872. It was said that this newspaper described the march as ludicrous and amusing, but that there would likely be no occasion to enforce the Ku Klux Act (using military force to suppress the KKK). We

---

[28] Cordelia Howard's death certificate notes that she was born on Oct. 14, 1873, but census records from 1900 and 1910 show her born in 1866 and married to John in 1882. This seems more likely given the ages of her children. She is recorded as "mulatto" meaning of mixed race, and as literate, and often working as a seamstress.

never had any encounter in our neighborhood with the KKK or even saw them. But there was much talk about demonstrations of hangings and killings in the Tidewater area of Norfolk and Newport News, Virginia. Word secretly travelled among the communities.[29]

My grandmother, smoking her corncob pipe, talked in very low tones to us about the Klan. She saw them set fire to colored homes and burn crosses they had made, all while the Klan knew they were watching. She remarked that the sheriff would not stop them. The Klan staged rallies, had marches and parades, and denounced immigrants.

I saw very little of my grandfather, John Howard. He was a farmer. He worked on a white man's farm and stayed there. He came home on Sundays for church or sometimes through the week. Whether he was born in slavery or not, I do not know. You never asked about slavery; it was one thing you learned as a child and it was repeated over and over to not ask that question.[30]

---

[29] No record of these events in New Market could be found, but the story is certainly plausible given that Virginia newspapers do show pro-KKK sentiment and attempts to organize it in the area in the early 1870s. See *Richmond Daily State Journal* (June 3, 1871), 1; *Daily State Journal* (Alexandria, VA: July 26, 1871 & March 29, 1872), 1; *Harrisonburg Rockingham Register* (Jan. 4, 1872), 3; and, *Alexandria Gazette* (Jan. 15, 1872), 3. And racial violence was certainly present in Harrisonburg at this time—Charlotte Davis, an African American woman, was lynched near Harrisonburg in March of 1878, accused of conspiring to burn down a white family's barn. Her body was left hanging for two days as a warning to others. See Tom Blair, "The Lynching of Charlotte Harris." Racial Terror: Lynching in Virginia. Available at: https://sites.lib.jmu.edu/valynchings/the-lynching-of-charlotte-harris/. In 2020 a historical marker about this incident was erected in Harrisonburg's Court Square.

[30] 1920 Census data show John Howard born in 1856 in Virginia, and that his parents were born in Virginia as well. Though illiterate, he was a skilled worker—a foreman of a dye works. He owned his house at 188 Effinger street that was valued at $750 (more expensive than most houses in that area) and the fact that his wife was not working

My maternal grandparents, Hezikiah and Willanna (Montgomery) Hughes,[31] lived in Pennsylvania by the time I was born, and did not come down often to see us. We would go there twice a year, and then my grandfather (who was black) and my grandmother (who was white) returned the visit. None of the younger children liked the big city; we were happy to go but glad to come back. We loved our wide-open spaces and the freedom to come and go. Our cousins liked it here in the Valley like we did. They always wanted to visit and not go back to the city.

Mixed marriages were avoided. When a person was even an eighth Negro blood, they were "black." My grandfather was a colored man and lived in the community, and my grandmother was white and lived out of the community.

My Aunt Minnie loved telling me stories and remarking, "do not tell," for example, that my mother's mother was white. Together my Aunt Minnie and my mother had the same father but not the same mother. Aunt Minnie's mother was African American. I did not understand how it could be—same father,

---

outside the home shows that he was financially stable. He does not appear in the Freedman's Bureau Records for Virginia, suggesting that though he was born during slavery, he was likely born free.

[31] Freedman records show that Hezekiah Hughes was born in 1859 in York Co., Virginia but lived in Harrisonburg by the late-1860s. 1900 and 1910 census records show that he married Anna Hughes (b. Feb. 1877) and that in 1900 they were living in Harrisonburg with two children, Minnie (b. May, 1893) and Fannie (b. Sept., 1894). The 1910 census suggests that Anna had a third child, William, in late-1900, but died in childbirth, and that Hezekiah married Willanna Montgomery from Rockbridge Co. shortly thereafter. She bore three children, but just two survived: Arlein (b. 1902) and Julia (b. 1906). In 1910 they were living among white neighbors with Minnie and William (Anna's children) and Arlein and Julia (Willanna's children) in their household. Hezekiah is listed as a day laborer in both 1900 and 1910. The census data lists Hezekiah, Anna, and Willanna all as "black" but it is quite possible given the white neighborhood they lived in (on West Market St. near the passenger train station) that Willanna was very light-skinned, causing the issues noted in the narrative.

different mothers. I was ten years of age and knew better than to ask questions. We were taught long ago to listen, not to question.

All I could do was wonder how that could be. It seemed forever before I found out. I learned one of my mother's sayings, which was true. When you asked a question, and our parents did not want to answer, the answer went like this, "if you live long enough, you will find the answer; it will come to you."

Young Doris with her Aunt Cuetta Howard and mother, Julia.

My mother's mother was my white grandmother. Now without anyone telling me, I could see why my mother was light complexioned, and I too, along with three of my siblings. Her father was African American, making her biracial. Marrying my father, who had parents that were mixed, he also was light complexioned. So in our family, four of us were light, and the two brown ones took after father.

My mother's mother, Willanna Hughes, was not a visitor in my childhood. I was never introduced to her. She died at an early age. It once was said that grandmother lived on Main Street in our city and also Pittsburgh, PA, but no one talked about her. I only know what my aunt said.

My mother's parents, the African American grandfather and the white grandmother, did not spend time together nor did they come to visit. I do know the "Jim Crow" law was very much in effect at that time. Should you be seen together there was punishment waiting. Those scenes were certainly avoided, as I never heard of any incidents. When you read the sign "No blacks and whites," it meant just that, no details, just the blunt way the sign would read. No marriage was performed between the races, yet contact was somehow made. If caught, there were consequences. You got fined or spent time in jail. If you did not have the fine, you were given a citation if you were black.

Virginia passed the Racial Integrity Act of 1924 which forbid marriage between "white" and "colored" people. The law defined "white" as having "no trace whatsoever of any blood other than Caucasian," putting in place the "one-drop rule"—regardless of physical appearance, anyone with any African, Asian, or Native American ancestry was considered "colored."

The Howard Family: (left to right) Sister Julia, Carmelita, Ernest, Alfred, mother Julia (on bike), brother Leo, Father Leo, and Doris (c. 1946)

My parents, Leo and Julia (Hughes) Howard, both grew up in Harrisonburg and were in school only until the seventh grade.[32] That was as far as their school went. Like other boys and girls, they were taught at home and went with family adults to their jobs as cooks, waiters, seamstresses, blacksmiths, horse trainers, farmers, and musicians.

My mother caught on very quickly and was taught by her aunts and uncles to serve, wait on tables, be a beautician, make party food, cater food, and other skills. She learned how to can

---

[32] Census and marriage records show that Leo (b. 1901) and Julia (b. 1902) were both born and raised in Harrisonburg and that they married on June 4, 1923. By 1930 they were renting the house next to Leo's parents at 190 Effinger St, and by 1940 they owned it. They had six children, Alfred (b. 1923), Carmelita (b. 1925), Julia (b. 1926), Doris (b. 1927), Leo Jr. (b. 1929), & Ernest (b. 1930). Leo worked as a housecleaner and Julia took in laundry—all the children attend school through high school.

vegetables and fruit by the bushel, which she in turn taught to her daughters. She also taught us girls at an early age to take care of infants, cook, sew, wash, iron, and care for declining seniors of all ages. My mother was a very firm, demanding, steadfast, determined, loving, and kind individual, making sure to get the job done and keep everyone on their toes.

From age five on up, everyone had a chore, including all my brothers and sisters and cousins too, if they lived with us. As time went on, your chores grew with you into something bigger or additional according to your age. My mother always said, "It is a right way and a wrong way. We gonna do the right way." She praised us when we were right and corrected us when wrong. All of our aunts and uncles could correct us too.

My mother was a very firm, positive person and when whites moved into our neighborhood, they were poorer than we were and usually dirty. My mother made a visit and made sure they understood they must have a clean house and clean children. With her help they did. My dad would say, "Julia, leave those folks alone." Sure enough, one day the father of the white family came over. He had been drinking, and he was knocking on the door. Dad answered the door. Mother was in the back yard, she asked, "Who is it?" Dad said, "The man next door." She said, "Let me at him." But when she got to the door, the man had run home. Everybody knew Ms. Julia. She was joyful and kind, loved everybody, but she took no foolishness.

My parents walked everywhere. They house cleaned for a living by appointment and mostly for Jewish people, as they paid more. There were very few Jews they did not work for. From Effinger Street to Madison College it was thirteen blocks one way. They walked there or in between every day to work. They also cleaned the three banks in downtown Harrisonburg every day (the National, the First National, and the Rockingham National). In the 1930s their wages were 35¢ to 50¢ an hour.

Family Photos

A family moment, with aunt Carmelita and her husband Weldon "Red Bundy, parents Leo and Julia Howard, Geraldine Howard (married to uncle Alfred Howard), Earnest Howard, and Doris and her husband Robert Harper.

Sunday afternoon tea at mother Julia Howard's home with cousins and friends. Doris is seated on the floor center left.

Family gathering in the backyard home of Julia and Leo Howard

Howard Family Portrait, Doris is on the back row right second from the end next to her brother Leo and nephew Jerry Howard. Below are her children, the "Three Bs": Bob, Belinda, and Bill. (c. 1965)

My father's work away from home was not just cleaning, but also as a gardener (what we would now call landscaping). He attended to several big homes with spacious grounds. At home he had three gardens, and he had each of us working in them. He planted and we watered, pulled weeds, and picked the vegetables when ready. Then as soon as the garden was finished, he would start another. Usually we had two plantings a year. He cared for the livestock whenever we had any.

Father Leo Howard, by the frame of the house he helped build for his family in the early 1920s, and mother Julia Hughes Howard at Rockingham Memorial Hospital where she worked as a cook's assistant.

I heard my Dad say one day that he went down the street to the Chesapeake and Ohio Railroad Station because he had heard they were hiring. When he got there, he read a sign outside that said, "Hiring." He inquired inside with the ticket agent who said "Boy, you know we don't hire 'Ns.' You better get away from here."

He and mother also housecleaned and catered for prominent families twice a year. At home I remembered my father's fine baking, cakes and pies—oooooh my!

Mother Julia Howard standing in front of brother Leo's "big bad Lincoln." Doris noted, "It was too big for me to drive!"

In 1947, my parents bought a Chevrolet car with the option that I, the only driver in the family, would teach my three sisters to drive. I did, though it was not an easy task. I learned to drive when I was twelve. The neighbor on the next street over had a car, and my sister's boyfriend taught me to drive his father's 1947 Ford. There was no tough restriction on having a permit. I drove without a license until I was twenty-three years old. A policeman stopped me one day, but he didn't give me a citation. He just said, "Get the license tomorrow," and I did. My cousin was right there with me, and I got it right away.

The family car in front of the house.

Family Reunions

Over the Blue Ridge Mountains and through the woods, back and forth on Highway 33 East, our families of brothers, sisters, cousins, nieces, and nephews were on our way at 8 A.M., always on Sunday, going to the annual family picnic in Madison, Virginia. Families came from West Virginia, Ohio, and Virginia.

In the 1930s, seems you could overload cars without a specific number of people, for we had three cars filled to the brim, as my mother would say. We had three big Model T Fords with open sides and no windows. How we stayed in I do not know, as there was no such thing as a seatbelt in those days. We could hardly wait to arrive over on the Blue Ridge Mountains to see and play with our cousins, to exchange games with them, to find out what they had different than what we had. We had games like: Little Sallie Walker, Farmer in the Dell, Hide and Seek, Hop Scotch, Jack Rocks, Jump Rope, Musical Chairs, and many others. We had so many because they lived more in the country than we considered ourselves.

We carried all kinds of cooked food. The usual way to carry fried chicken was in tin tubs that were used to wash clothes in, covered with a big kitchen table cloth and tied down. There were homemade breads, cakes, pies, leafy vegetables, pots of string beans, jams, jelly, peanut butter, apple butter, potato salad, cooked collards, cabbage, homemade pickles, applesauce, apples fried, stewed, and baked every way imaginable, peaches too in the same different ways. Crisp fried bacon would be on the tables outside when we arrived along with more of the same foods we brought. Country ham was plentiful, as well as ribs and smoked meats.

One particular container I looked for was the ice cream freezer. There were oh so many kinds of ice cream: vanilla, strawberry, chocolate, raspberry, cherry, banana, and peach. Those stood out more than any others. I remember the long tables in the front yard all covered with white table cloths. When dinner was ready, the cow bell rang. Children were all fed and then the adults. We ate outside and should it rain, the tables of food would be covered with kitchen table cloths, and whenever the rain stopped, we ate. There was no such thing as paper products. We ate at the picnic tables with china and silverware.

We children were so busy running and playing with our cousins of which we had new and old ones. We had the best times of our lives. We entertained ourselves with each other, never distracting the older members from their conversations. There were new games we had to learn from each other. That kept us busy and being all family, we knew the rules and respect you paid each other, so we played well together. Fun, fun, nothing but fun! All families used the same discipline and never had a disagreement. Prayer and peace prevailed at all times.

Ice cream came at the end of the day when it was time to go home. Ice cream was eaten in a bowl. There were no cones then. If so, they were too expensive to buy. We never had cones. Goodbyes were not easy, but when time came to go, it was said. We usually arrived back home around 7 P.M. It would still be daylight as it was a two-hour ride home, and oh how grateful we were to ride and sleep all the way.

Chapter 4
CHILDHOOD MEMORIES

The Howard family (my family) lived on upper Effinger Street, kitty cornered from Effinger School. When it rained long and hard, we knew Blacks Run at the bottom of Effinger would rise and overflow, flooding the same families' properties over and over. When the water receded, the families would return and clean up the mess as the landlord would not take care of it. All the children loved to play in the muddy, dirty, unclean waters, and why we never got sores or infections, I'll never know. There were no swimming pools.

Aunt Cuetta, brothers-in-laws Weldon "Red" and Rawley Bundy (brothers who married Doris's sisters, Carmelita and Julia), and cousin Jane at Rawley Springs.

Our family and friends went to Rawley Springs about twelve miles on Route 33 west of our city to picnic and swim. My parents would call our senior cousins who had a big car with big windows (a 1938 Buick) and another car (a 1935 Plymouth) to take us to the water. We could also fish. A lunch was packed, and away we'd go and stay all day. First we'd clear the weeds and trees each time we'd go. Then the same space got bigger and bigger. Food, fun, games, and wading in the water for few of us could swim. My cousins were probably the only ones that knew how to swim. My parents never could.

Going Down Town

My Aunt Minnie Stewart (my mother's half-sister) took me downtown one day. We walked the seven blocks from Effinger Street to Main Street. When we got to Elizabeth Street, she took my hand and held it tight until we got to East Market. As soon as we got to East Market, I looked toward the court house and said, "Aunt Minnie, I want a drink of water." From the fountain in front of the courthouse yard, white people stepped on a pedal to draw water to drink. She would squeeze my hand and shake her head, "No." How was a seven-year-old to know she could not have a drink of water when everybody else was drinking? The sign said: *White Only*. I still did not know.

1930s Postcard of Harrisonburg's Court Square.

Baseball

There would be free baseball practice at the city park on Sundays. We would gather our bats and balls and all of our baseball paraphernalia and off to the diamond we would go. We even brought our cheerleading squad with us, fresh water, and maybe lemonade. We would start our game and maybe get halfway through, and here would come the white players to make us leave.

Little did I know my future husband, Robert Lee Harper, would be an early baseball player with the Homestead Giants in the Shenandoah Valley in the 1950s.

Doris's husband, Robert Lee Harper is in the center row left seated at end.

They put up signs all around the diamond that said, "No Niggers, No Jews, No Dogs," and our dogs were plentiful and ran wild in those days (there were no dog permits or licenses). The police would then come and break up fights and make us leave. This was on a public diamond. If the white players were there first, we didn't bother them.

Riding an Airplane

1946 photo of Hartman Field. It closed in 1953 and today its runway is Hartman Drive. See Randall B. Jones, Hartman Airfield: Harrisonburg's Runway to Flight *(2006).*

In the 1940s on Sunday afternoon, from 1:00–5:00 P.M., my sister Julia and I along with my two favorite cousins, Louise and Arnold, would go to Hartman Airport Hanger near Eastern Mennonite School for an airplane ride over the city. It cost one dollar for a one-hour trip. My sister Julia was two years older than I, and I would keep egging her on so she would give in. I reminded her how hard we had to work to get the two dollars—we went to the store for grandma, and for Aunt Minnie we got coal from the coal house and put it in the bin behind the cook stove in the kitchen. We brought in wood for Aunt Minnie; we carried water for Aunt Bessie; we fed her dog, walked him, and gave him a bath. See, everybody could pay you but Mother. That was a big no-no. It didn't matter how much she wanted done, you could not charge. And for others, whatever anyone gave you was OK—no charging. Sometimes they would say, "I don't have any money," and you'd have to do it anyway.

Louise and Arnold said they were going to ride, but when we got there, they said they were not; they had changed their minds. Then I had to hug my sister and promise her something. Finally, she gave in, and up the steps into the four-passenger plane we went. She was in front as I wanted to make sure she was not backing out. Poor sister had tears in her eyes but a big grin on her face. I was well pleased. After I strapped her in, she had her eyes closed and kept them closed.

Finally, the plane started moving. I was watching her every move. The plane began to lift up, up, up, and she got tickled and was smiling, but the eyes stayed closed. She wouldn't look out. I sang some funny songs, and she was enjoying them. I watched her closely, and the smiles stayed. Then we started down. Oh me! I felt the change up. Whoa, I felt a little woozy. "I can't get sick, Lord," I begin to pray, "Lord, you got to help me through this. I haven't been up here either. Don't leave me Lord." Things calmed down, and I forgot I was on the way down after looking at Julia enjoying herself.

We hit the ground smoothly, and my sister's eyes popped open quick. She was happy and when we got out, she was telling Louise and Arnold how much fun she had and how much they missed a big ride. We went home, and she was still rattling off about the good time. Oh, I was so pleased!

In 1943 Doris's Aunt Cuetta invited her to visit her in Rochester, NY where her husband was an airplane pilot

Two Sundays later I asked everybody again. My sister said "oh yes," and my two cousins Louise and Arnold said "count us in," so we all started saving our work money to go. We went to the airport, everybody laughing and singing. We got there but as I started to buy the tickets, but my cousins said they weren't going. I looked at Louise's big eyes watering up and she said "I don't think I want to go today." That was our last attempt to ride. The old airport office has since been replaced by a Family Dollar store on Chicago Avenue off of Mount Clinton Pike.[33]

Doris Howard at age 16.

---

[33] According to Randall B. Jones *Hartman Airfield: Harrisonburg's Runway to Flight* (2006), "In 1939 [Dan] Hartman leased a 44 acre family farm to establish an airport. It was located northwest of Harrisonburg, just outside the city limits, situated between the town & the Mennonite community of Park View." More specifically, the hanger was located between Chicago Avenue and Hartman Drive. It operated from 1939–1953. For more information see the central Virginia section of Paul Freeman's website, *Abandoned and Little-known Airfields:* www.airfields-freeman.com/VA/Airfields_VA_C.htm

Visiting The Poor House

There was an old folks' home of homeless persons who were unable to work and had no place to call home, or they had a disability and no income.[34] They lived on Pleasant Valley Road, south of the city, off Route 11. In the early 1940s, Effinger Street (where I lived in Newtown) was some five miles north of the home. On no special Saturday, a group of eight or ten of us would get together and hike and plan to go to visit and entertain the folk with singing, dancing, Bible stories, and prayer. Saturday was a good day as there was no train running, so we could walk the rails all the way from Newtown to the old folks' home. We packed a lunch of crackers, water, sometimes lemonade, apples, grapes, whatever fruit was in season, and cookies one parent would make. We always got approval from our parents to go, and they encouraged us to do so. We called it our special duty and felt proud to visit and entertain them, showing off our talent making the old folks happy and rejoicing.

The old folks' home was a place for anyone with no income, no family, or no place to call home. They were housed there by the city, all expenses paid. Churches would also come in to see them and bring goodies. We would stay as late as we could but had to get back before dark. We brought buckets along with us to pick asparagus, rhubarb, berries of any kind, chinquapins—any food growing we picked. Our parents knew we would come home with vegetables, fruit, and wild flowers. Following the rails, we could not get lost as they went right back to Newtown. There was never any misdemeanor from adults as to kidnap, rape, or molestation.

---

[34] The Rockingham County Poorhouse was built in 1870 and closed in 1961. It was on the ground currently occupied by Massanutten Technical Center and Pleasant Valley Elementary School. The main house, a two-story brick building with a wing for males and a wing for females, stood almost where the current Harrisonburg Electric Co. building on Pleasant Valley Road stands today. Serena Hepner, "Gone and Forgotten." (2002) From the *North Fork Journal*, http://freepages.genealogy.rootsweb.ancestry.com/~pvaca/gone.htm .

Seems like nothin' like that occurred in our day or very rarely. To keep safe was one reason we all traveled in groups to movies, church, school, parties etc. Each household taught the same rules.

Doris Jean Howard married Robert Lee Harper on June 4, 1950. The reception was at her parents' house at 194 Effinger St.

Chapter 5
PEOPLE IN THE NEIGHBORHOOD

Two-Penny George[35]

Sometimes we hiked out North Main Street on Route 11 until we got to the intersection of Mt. Clinton Pike. There, we bore to the left and went down a road with no name to a farm at the end of the road. It was a big farm with lots of livestock, cats, dogs, all kinds of animals, ponies, horses, and cows. We knew the family that lived there. They welcomed us every time we came. We met them at the Gay Street Mission Church (Mennonite) in the city. As soon as we arrived, we would wash our hands and have warm milk and crackers, then jelly, bread, and butter.

---

[35] Census data from 1900–1940 reveals that this man's name was actually George Steele (born c. 1886), the son of John Steele (born c. 1832). In 1900, the Steele family lived with Clara Fields, a 70-year-old black woman in Harrisonburg. From 1910 through 1950, George lived as a lodger and servant (census records list him as both) with Elverton and Margie Shands, a white family that owned both a large farm at 1423 Mt. Clinton Pike and a big house in downtown Harrisonburg at 544 S. Main St. It seems one of George's primary duties was to walk the 5-mile round-trip between these properties, bringing eggs and milk from the farm to the house in town. Elverton Shands was a prominent lawyer, business man, and farmer. After he died in 1935, George continued to live with Margie Shands until her death in 1950. After that time, he lived with Roberta Webb, a black woman who cared for elderly homeless black men, compensated for her service by the city. According to Webb's grandson, Earl Franklin Jr., George lived with them until 1965 when they moved out of Harrisonburg. There are many local stories about "Two-Penny George," and they suggest that he was autistic—eccentric but kind—a well-loved local character. He was commemorated after his death with the naming of "Two Penny Lane," a street that runs above Eastern Mennonite University close to the Shands' Mt. Clinton Pike farm.

On the farm was a grown man named George Sands [sic]. His parents were deceased. The farm family had also raised George's father, who had been a slave with them. Now George had been homeless, and they took him to raise. George liked pennies and every Saturday George walked into the city. He'd ask people he'd meet for two pennies, no nickel. Too heavy he'd say, just two pennies. If you didn't have two pennies, he'd walk away and ask the next person. This went on for years as long as I can remember. George would take the pennies home and put them in a bag and keep saving them.

He was a very beautiful blue-black skin man and had a bright smile. When I would travel into downtown Harrisonburg with my mother or father he would always be by the courthouse standing, when you went in or came out. He would smile and ask for a penny. My mother and father would always give him a penny, and he would thank them with a kind smile with white teeth and clear blight eyes. As us kids got older we would love to see him downtown and give him a penny, just to see his wonderful happy smile. Time passed and we didn't see him anymore. The story in Newtown goes that he died and that he was buried on the farm and that the family that raised him put him away very lavishly.

Mr. Freeze[36]

Mr. Freeze on Kelley Street kept a big garden and had a vegetable stand always in his yard. He lived in a shack on the property although he did not own the land but had lived there a long time. Not married, no family, just Mr. Freeze. He had fruit trees—apple, pear, peach—and lots of grape harbors (we called them). He canned his food and fruit for winter. In the winter he sold wood he cut and put in bundles on his wagon and would go to the railroad tracks and pick up lumps of coal that dropped from moving trains that passed through the city. He had a little four-

---

[36] "Mr. Freeze" may be J.R. Freeze. The 1940 census shows him as a 61-year-old white man living with his wife, Alice (also 61) on E. Johnson St. (near Kelley St.) at an address recorded as "0" which suggests an un-official residence, not house, and among black neighbors. See: www.familysearch.org/ark:/61903/1:1:VR1R-TV3.

wheeled homemade red wagon, and he had put sides on it. He pulled it all over Newtown. Mr. Freeze was about four feet tall, a very small frail little fellow, happy and smiling, always cheerful, very few words, just smiles.

Doc Dickerson[37]

If we did use a doctor, we ran to get help from "Doc" Dickerson. Dr. Eugene A. Dickerson lived on the corner of Wolfe and Mason Streets, was married to Leona, and had three children: Eva, Eugene, and Austin. He was the physician for Newtown and all blacks in the county. He worked long hours until late at night. There were few phones and thus plenty of people running in on his porch saying, "Doc we need you right away." He would respond quickly. He got the name Doc Dickson very soon. You could call in or walk in, no matter. You always had to wait. There was only one white doctor in the city you could see—Dr. Harshbarger. He lived on South Mason Street (twelve blocks south). His office was also in his home.[38] The pair worked together

---

[37] Dr. Eugene A. Dickerson was born in Charlottesville and earned his A.B. at Virginia Normal and Collegiate Institute (now Virginia State University) and his medical degree from Leonard Medical College in Raleigh, NC. He did post-doctoral work at Howard University, and then worked in West Virginia and briefly in Staunton, Virginia before coming to Harrisonburg in 1910. He married Leona Anderson of Staunton who had graduated from Morgan College (now Morgan State University) and did further studies at Fisk University. This highly-educated African-American couple owned a large house at 202 Mason St. out of which Dr. Dickerson practiced. Leona died in 1924, leaving Dr. Dickerson with their three children: Eugene Jr. (b. 1908), Eva (b. 1913) and Austin (b. 1922). Dr. Dickerson continued practicing medicine in Harrisonburg into the 1950s; he died in 1955. For more information see Dale MacAllister, "Prominent Harrisonburg Physician Dr. Eugene Dickerson." *Heritage Museum Newsletter* of the Harrisonburg-Rockingham Historical Society (Winter, 2016) 38, no. 1: 8-9.

[38] 1940 census records show that Dr. Jacob C. Harshbarger (b. 1901) was a young white doctor in Harrisonburg who lived with his wife

in the practice and were good friends. There were also several midwives. Babies in the early 1900s were born at home, so the midwives were busy.

Dr. Stratton was another colored medical doctor and had offices out of his home from the 1930s to 1970s.[39] That was a familiar practice then; it was something the law allowed or they had not made a ruling. Dr. Stratton made house calls, and when midwives did not deliver babies, he did. Midwives didn't go to hospitals to deliver babies. They were homebound servants.

Doc Dickerson had one plum, one crabapple, one green apple in his yard. We kids had a picnic whenever we could. He never used them and that made it better for all in the neighborhood. Doc was a great doctor, kind, gentle personality, patient with seniors and children as his patients, yet he did not want kids in his fruit trees, especially the plum tree. We felt he didn't use them and we could not leave them alone. Doc said we broke his tree limbs, but our little group did not because we always sent Little Happy, our cousin, to the top. Because he was so tiny and fast, up he could go.

Sometimes we were lucky. Doc would be out on call, and we could be in and out before he got home. See he had the biggest and the sweetest plums in the whole Newtown. There were always plenty on the ground, but we wanted to shake and get more. His porch was all across the front of the house, and in the summer he had morning glory blooming around it. In the evening, the sun beamed down, but it was nice and cool on the porch. Often times we were so busy looking at the big plums we did not pay attention to whether his car was in the drive. In fact, sometimes it was in the garage. We'd sneak up and start shaking the tree, and he'd holler, "I'm going to call your mother. I know who you are." Why would

---

Patience and daughter Carolyn at his house/office at 594 Mason St. just three blocks from Dr. Dickerson.

[39] 1940 census records list Henry A. Stratton as a "medical" worker with his own private practice and show that he came from South Carolina and lived with his wife Catherine and daughter Sylvia Ann at his house/office at 237 Broad St. Other Newtown residents remember him working primarily as a dentist.

he say that? We really were afraid to go home. Sure enough, the message beat us home plus there was plum juice on our clothes and the purple lips were showing. Mother always had to send us out for the switches and that day it was six of us, counting two cousins and Little Happy. We all got a whipping. You see, in Newtown, families as well as neighbors had permission to punish your child as mentioned before.

Doc Dickerson lost a son in his early adult life. His daughter Eva graduated from Virginia State College, Petersburg, Virginia, an all-black college. His oldest graduated from Howard University, an all-black school in Washington, D.C. After their mother passed away, they continued in college, graduated, came back and forth to see their father, and soon they both were married and had families.

Doc passed away at a ripe old age of seventy-six in 1955, and he bequeathed his home to the Masonic Order of Fraternal Brothers. The Brothers of the craft embraced the gift with full honor, and today after eight decades, the historic home stands out in the community, still being used by the Loyal Order in memory of Dr. Eugene A. Dickerson.

Roberta Webb

Mrs. Roberta Webb, a school teacher, was married to John Webb (though she was married she was still called Miss Webb). Besides having three daughters—Nancy, Peggy, and Ada—Miss Webb took in boarders and taught school in Rockingham County. Miss Webb drove a 1930 Buick and kept it in the garage where it stayed clean and polished. She and her family lived on Broad Street around the corner from our home on Effinger Street. We could see her house from where we lived. The Webbs, like the Howards, had the only telephone on their entire block, although Miss Webb charged 5¢ to use her phone. In using the phone it was always business. Nobody made social calls. Even our parents never played or fooled around on the phone. I really cannot remember my sisters and brothers ever using the phone and it hardly rang, but we always had a telephone.

Miss Webb taught her daughters to sing and play the piano. They sang as a trio all over Newtown and the county. One daughter, Peggy, sang high soprano and sounded like an opera singer. After graduating from high school, she enrolled in Hesston College in Hesston, Kansas. After she graduated, she came home and was married, and after having a son, finished her bachelor's degree at Eastern Mennonite College, becoming its first black graduate in 1954—graduating a few months before the *Brown v. Topeka Board of Education* case struck down segregated education. Her other two sisters also attended college. Their father became suddenly ill and died of tuberculosis, which was very common in those days and had no treatment or cure. Miss Webb and the girls attended Broad Street Mennonite Church, although Miss Webb joined before the girls finished high School. When the girls went off to school, Miss Webb moved to Mennonite Town (now Park View, a section in the northwest of the city). When she moved, Miss Webb bequeathed her home to the Mennonite Church.

Roberta Webb, "a master teacher," of both academic and practical skills showing children from the Newtown community how to wash clothes.

Before moving to Mennonite Town, Miss Webb was active in Newtown Community, teaching children to sing and to play the piano. She had recitals at the end of the year and did so out of her home. They performed at our three black churches and all the other black churches in the county. Along with her boarders, she fed the needy folks (as they were called) and cared for the sickly in Newtown. She also owned and operated the first day care center in Northeast Harrisonburg for Blacks. Her aged mother, Miss Morgan, was her "chief cook and bottle washer."

Roberta Webb and daughters Nancy, Margaret (Peggy), and Ada
(c. 1943)
Image courtesy of Eastern Mennonite University Historical Library

Wednesday night was Prayer Meeting at Miss Webb's house. Every Wednesday people would be sitting outside on the porch and in the grass even though there were churches with prayer meetings. Miss Webb always had her own group. Born in 1889, Miss Webb expired at the age of 101 years old. Later the Newtown Day Care Center was named The Roberta Webb Center, in her honor, and is very much alive and busy with a full attendance to this day.[40]

Roberta Webb, daughter Nancy, husband Frank, and son Earl Franklin Jr. in front of their house on Broad Street, very close to the Harpers' house.

---

[40] For more on the life of Roberta Webb see Melody Pannell, "Remembering Roberta: Let Her Legacy Live On." Mennonite Mission Network, (March 24, 2021). Available at: www.mennonitemission.net/blog/Remembering-Roberta-Let-her-legacy-live-on

Chapter 6
COMMUNITY

Bundy's Boy Band in 1945. Weldon "Red" Bundy (Doris's sister Carmeltia's husband) was the lead trumpet player of the Bundy's Boy Band; (back row far right). Her brother Earnest Howard played saxophone (third row right). Her friend Duffy Smith was a trumpeter and the band's youngest member (front row, second from the left).

Music and Dance

The Bundy's Boys Band was the only African-American marching band throughout the valley. The Band was unique in that its performances included traditional march music as well as popular jazz-influenced music by Count Basie and Duke Ellington during the 1940s and 1950s.

In the 1930s there were no televisions and few radios but always group-singing, soloists, duets, quartets in practice at school or church, mass choirs all over the neighborhood. In our northeast community we had all kinds of singers, the young learning from the older generation, always forming another group. Anyone who could dance was free to teach others to do so. For example, my sister was taught by my cousin to tap dance and grew up on stage at school, church, or the downtown theater. She was many times at our local theater on Saturday. Another cousin played the drums like nobody else could. He accompanied my sister for her sessions. At the movies their performance was an extra feature during intermission. We held regular variety shows as a way to stimulate the younger fans and create a new beginning, teaching and encouraging others to perform and to excel.

Homemade instruments were made from tin, wood, metal, paper, and anything that made a sound was tested, like pots and pans, wash boards, bottles of different sizes, wire strung up, sticks of different shapes and sizes, rubber balls. The piano had to be real, however, and was often put on a board of wheels and moved from place to place. It was not unusual to see a piano rolling down the road being directed by several persons day and night in Newtown. Sometimes a band started with one instrument, then another and another. Before long, a complete group was performing live music to hear on the street, in a restaurant, empty building, or whatever was available.

Singing has been the backbone of our communities. I say that to mean we sang at an early age. It was our culture. Dancing and singing made happiness, made us cheerful, made us forget any sadness, any sorrow. Physically and mentally we were blessed. Everyone young and old would join in the celebrations whether in church, at home, or in the streets.

Our elders sang the old Negro spirituals like "Go down Moses" which was one of my favorites.[41] Elders often sang stirring

---

[41] "Go Down, Moses" has a long history among Virginia's African American community. It was the first spiritual ever printed, published in 1862 as "O, Let My People Go." It was written down by Lewis Lockwood, a white minister who heard "Contrabands" (enslaved people who escaped to freedom during the Civil War) singing it at Fort Monroe in Hampton, Virginia in 1861.

lyrics from other songs as well, such as: "Oh, Mary don't you weep, don't you mourn. Pharaoh's army got drowned, Oh Mary don't you weep." And, "When I get to heaven, going to sing and shout! Nobody there for to turn me out."

"Joshua fought the Battle of Jericho" was a song which we understood in our own lives—that there are times when you need to bring down the walls of Jim Crow. This idea was also expressed in the Civil Rights anthem, "We Shall Overcome":

> We shall overcome some day...
> Deep in our heart, we do believe,
> we shall overcome someday.
> We'll walk hand and hand....
> We are not afraid....
> We shall have peace someday....
> We shall overcome someday.[42]

These are songs that Grandma Cordelia and family members sang to us. We did not work in the cotton fields here in Virginia, but we knew the songs they would sing. We learned the songs, repeating after our elders. We didn't have books; we just listened to them. The same song would be sung at church and all would clap and even shout. Children did not shout, but the preacher and our elders did.

Songs were also sung during wash day. Throughout the summer the washboard was busy in the backyard. Monday was washday, and the three tin tubs were under the shade tree. The three long clotheslines were empty and waiting. The big black kettle in the middle of the yard had fire burning under it to keep the water hot and boiling for the clothes. Mother and my three

---

[42] "We Shall Overcome" has deep roots in the black musical tradition,— its music and words appear in varying formats in several songs dating back to the first recorded spirituals. The version commonly sung today emerged during protests beginning in the 1940s and Pete Seeger's version of the song became a standard of the Civil Rights Movement of the 1950–1960s.

sisters were busy sorting and bringing clothes out to wash when someone started one of Grandma Cordelia's favorite songs,

> Lift every voice and sing, till earth and heaven ring,
> ring with the harmonies of liberty;
>
> Let our rejoicing rise, high as the listening skies, let
> it resound loud as the rolling sea.[43]

With all the help mother had, if it was a nice sunny day, clothes were hung to dry and brought back into the house, folded, and put away. Also, the sheets were laundered and dried and put back onto the beds. So, wash day was a big busy day.

Again, singing was a relief from Jim Crow, which was ugliness, bitterness, and unpleasant spices of life that we endured from the opposite race. The laws of the land were to separate us, but Jim Crow laws had no bearing on singing and dancing among ourselves. We were to ourselves—separate from whites. We felt free.

---

[43] "Lift Every Voice and Sing" was a poem written by James Weldon Johnson (eventual head of the N.A.A.C.P.) in 1900, and later set to music by his brother, J. Rosamond Johnson, and published as a song in 1905. In 1919 the N.A.A.C.P. designated it "the Negro national anthem."

Songs My Grandmother Used to Sing

1. We're Marching on To Zion
2. When Peace Like a River
3. At the Cross
4. I Will Trust In the Lord
5. Jesus Loves Me
6. Lord I'm Coming Home
7. Jesus Keep Me Near the Cross
8. Battle Hymn of the Republic
9. We'll Overcome Someday
10. Jesus Loves the Little Children
11. Farther Along
12. I Know Who Holds Tomorrow
13. He Lives
14. His Eye Is on the Sparrow
15. I Shall Not Be Moved
16. Oh, How I Love Jesus
17. No, Not One!
18. Stand By Me
19. Where He Leads Me
20. In the Garden
21. Just a Closer Walk with Thee
22. Leaning on the Everlasting Arms
23. We'll Understand By and By
24. Yield Not to Temptation
25. I Surrender All
26. Love Lifted Me
27. My Soul's Been Anchored in de Lord
28. I Couldn't Hear Nobody Pray
29. Sometimes I Feel Like a Motherless Child
30. Let Us Break Bread Together
31. Freedom Train a-Comin'
32. Have a Little Talk with Jesus
33. Hush, Hush, Somebody's Callin' My Name
34. Swing Low, Sweet Chariot
35. Standin' in the Need of Prayer

36. Go Down, Moses
37. Deep River
38. Roll, Jordan, Roll
39. Do, Lord, Remember Me
40. Wade in the Water
41. This Little Light of Mine
42. Steal Away
43. Study War No More
44. Mary, Don't You Weep, Don't You Mourn
45. Joshua fought the Battle of Jericho

The 1964 Lucy F. Simms School Choir. Doris's children Belinda Harper (back row left on the end), and Bob Harper (below Belinda second from the end), where members of the Simms School choir. The school song was "Dear Lucy Simms." Ms. Mary Awkard Fairfax and Mr. Nathaniel Moore were the directors.

Indians and Minstrels

For three years or more every summer, a dozen or so of full-blooded Catawba Indians (or so my dad said) came to Joseph's field at Washington and Main St. and put up tents and stayed two weeks. The grounds were already fenced in. We could stand outside and look but not go in. They did their war dances, wore their native dress, had ceremonies, went to the woods, and came back with wild animals they'd killed, which they skinned and cooked right before our eyes. School was out for us so we had free time; we'd go up to the campgrounds and stay all day. Our mothers had to send for us, but we would all be in a group together from our street and that made it safe. They spoke their native language, washed clothes, and cared for the many children running around. They always had a big feast at the end of the day with prayer, singing, and dancing. Only a certain few came out to do errands. We never communicated or socialized in any way. Everyone obeyed the rules and there was no crossing over into their camp at any time. After two weeks, they loaded their covered wagons and disappeared until the next year.

We also had minstrels, a big sideshow of all black entertainment. The main and favorite one was Silas Green (1904–1957). They came from New Orleans. This show had an all-black cast of men and women with jokes, singing, dancing, and beautiful costumes. They called it "minstrels" because it ministered to people. Some were comedians in black faces. There was one particular field on Broad Street that was kept cleared away for Silas Green.

Billboards were sent ahead as advertisements went up early. They had a huge tent; it seemed the largest I had ever seen. They had a band that played really professionally. It cost children 25¢, adults 50¢, and it was the same price every year. It was a one-night stand. After Harrisonburg, they were off to Staunton. They went early the next day before dawn. Silas Green was a big hit with our community because they had lots of good talent, pretty women, fancy dresses, and many popular actors that were famous. The usual ballpark goodies were sold as well as all kinds of souvenirs. It was fun for all.

Circus Day

Circus Day in Harrisonburg, c. 1900—contributed by Harriet Welch[1]

---

[1] http://usgwarchives.net/va/photo/harrisonburg/circus.jpg

On Circus Day, the Big Parade would begin at 10:00a.m. sharp. There were fire trucks, buggies, wagons, dogs, fancy dressed horses, and elephants that came in on the coal car of the train. At 4:00a.m. my daddy went down to see the unloading. School was out because this was Circus Day. Big Posters were placed all over Newtown whenever the Circus was coming to town.

One year, being single, I was designated to chaperone the eight little nieces and nephews aged four years, six years, eight years and ten years. Their mamas put them up to say "Aunt Doris, Aunt Doris did you know it is a Circus in town?" Seems like a lot, but the ten-year-olds were very helpful. The biggest job was preparing the eight sandwich bags with names on each bag and a dollar in change in each bag. Oh me. It cost 25¢ to get in, 15¢ for popcorn right away, 25¢, for the show in the big tent, 15¢ colored ice (frozen Kool-Aid I guess), and 20¢ for cotton candy or a caramel apple on the way home.

As the Big Show got ready to start, we got our seats down front, and I asked the question "Who's got to go to the restroom?" If nobody said anything, in we'd go, jumping and happy. The ten-year-olds had the six-year-olds' hands. I was holding hands with the four-year-olds, and the eight-year-olds were walking nicely in front of me. We got great seats down low, and all were seated. Exactly ten minutes under the big tent and the six-year-olds needed to go to the restroom. Oh me, all the crowd screaming, up I got with the six-year-olds and set off to the portie toilets, leaving the four-year-olds and the eight-year-olds with the ten-year-olds. We go only to find a line and five toilets busy. The line moved very quickly and we dashed back and the Big Show had not started. Great! We were glad.

The clowns were running and jumping, shaking hands with people, cart-wheeling, dancing and tossing the ball in the air. We got back to the seats and the eight-year-old had to go, so the trip was repeated with only a shorter line at the potty. Back into the tent we went just in time to see the lady high up on the trapeze climbing the ladder. We found our seats and here came the great big elephants, eight of them, and three little ones, the clowns running along the side. The band played loudly while everybody was clapping. The children were happy and laughing.

The ponies came next, and then the horses were prancing. Lots of fancy dogs were dressed up in clothing, monkeys were riding on the elephants, there were zebras and two giraffes, three lions rode in a cage, and the circus people ran behind. Our seats were perfect. The children could see everything. The noise rolled, and so did the fun.

Soon it was time to start home. We got a ride over, but we had to walk the five blocks back home. The candy apples and the cotton candy had to stay in the bag. No one could eat another bite. The ten-year-olds had to piggy-back the four-year-olds, and each one of them went to sleep on their backs, holding on good around their necks. Holding hands with the six-year-olds was no problem. Being girls, they were easy to control. The eight- year-olds were like two soldier buddies, one trying to outdo the other in remembering the stunts and acts at the circus.

Real Soldiers

Before the war ended in 1945, we would hear by word of mouth that an army convoy was coming through. The soldiers had so many hours, stopping for a break, and we would be preparing for entertainment. They never spent the night. They would come at noon and stay 'til midnight maybe, and then away they went. At that time, we had a designated place called the U.S.O. Center on Wolfe Street in the city. There would be dancing in the street so streets would be blocked off. Big army trucks would be all over the area, not in Newtown, but on Wolfe Street where our activities were held in the dance hall, churches, U.S.O., restaurants, community center, and especially the barber shop. There was a curfew for the younger persons, and the patrol was visible. The soldiers passing through went on for several years. Virginia had several camps close to our town. The soldiers would be training in the higher elevation of West Virginia, and their route to Camp Lee near Richmond took them through Harrisonburg. Addresses would be exchanged and writing soldiers' letters was a popular topic of conversation. Each wanted to see who could get the most addresses, and we would write them.

I was not in the U.S. Military but my sister Julia was. It was so exciting to put on her uniform. The entire Newtown community was so proud of her being the first Black woman from Harrisonburg in the United States Army.

Doris's sister, Julia Howard (sitting on arm of chair) served in the Women's Army Auxiliary Corp (WAAC) during WWII.

My three brothers each served in the United States Service. My mother signed up one brother underage, and the other two were 18 years old, the proper age to join. Before the age of 18, black boys were dropping out of school. They felt they were not learning anything, became disinterested, and then would find a job and go to work or join the Armed Forces of the USA.

Many men from Newtown fought in WWII. Pictured here (left to right). Back Row: Jerry Williams, Elon Rhodes, Bobo Sampson, Joe Nickens, Edgar Johnson, Melvin Stevens, Madison Brown.
Front Row: John Howard (Doris's brother), Bill Brown, Lorenza Strother, Landis Brown, Wilmer Byrd.

When World War II broke out, the young men found they could join the army if their parents would sign. So many quit school and joined the Service, only to find Jim Crow laws existing there too. There was name-calling (the "N" word ranked very high), spitting on people, cursing, fighting, and lots of unkindness. My brothers looked above it all saying you learned to live with it and search for happiness. Two brothers served four years and one served twenty-six years. All received high school diplomas at graduation because one outstanding feature of the U.S. Services at that time was that you could join the forces without having completed high school, but then you had to attend school and get your GED while in the service.

My second husband, Hezekiah Allen, had a nephew who was only fourteen years old and he had three fifteen-year-old buddies, tall and healthy. They looked like eighteen-year-olds. They decided among themselves to enlist in the military services of our country in 1945, in Huntington, WV. The boys had planned between themselves to not tell their parents. They went to their school in Huntington one day, made the first class and skipped the second one. They left school and went down the alley to the selective service office, signed up for the army corps, and were given a card with a serial number on it. They were told to take the card to the train station and give it to the conductor on the train.

Since they had the papers already signed, the conductor accepted them and said you are headed for Camp Atterbury, IN, to the United States Army Air Corps. When they got there the boys were told that they had seven days to get their business straight before shipping out, but they did not have any business, and away they went. World War II was on. Uncle Sam was taking young males without physicals and no signing from parents. Just pass a written test and you were in.

The first round of Jim Crow was at Boot Camp—whites over here and blacks over there—separate. They heard a lot of the "N" word and got into lots of fights. It was double hard as the whites were all their commanders, and they never got a break. Blacks did the dirty work and worked overtime, anytime, all the time. They got left over food or no food, but they stuck together.

The boys finished Boot Camp, went to Florida and were to board a bus to Pensacola, but the white soldiers would not let them board the bus. That bus left, and they said our bus was coming. Another bus came that had a sign in front saying, "Negro Troops." More Jim Crow. My nephew said, "We will not board," and they would not. So the driver removed the sign.

The boys were inducted into a unit called the 555th Parachute Infantry Battalion, also known as the Triple Nickels. They were known in the United States Air Corps as an all-black Parachute

Platoon. There, Jim Crow was certainly alive. My nephew said, "We continued to be picked on. We were tossed back and forth with unnecessary orders, still having food problems, never up front, always in the rear, and still we were happy to serve in the service of our country."

My nephew was a very hard worker at basic training. He was taken under a superior officer's wing and given a special assignment over his peers and carried it out well. Upon graduation, everyone became a private 1st class but my nephew became a Corporal. His buddies reminded him that his light complexion pushed him forward.

Their unit was shipped to Greensboro, NC, then on to Fort Dix, NJ, and straight on to Naples, Italy. Overseas, their all-black unit ran into problems with white soldiers in the still segregated United States military. Jim Crow was still alive. Their troops were housed in the swampy area while white troops were in barracks on the hill. They were given menial tasks to perform and they were a unit without a home base. It took three years following desegregation in 1947 till the Triple Nickels became the 555th Parachute Infantry Regiment. They were finally allowed to jump. It was Good Friday, 1951, in Korea, when their first black paratrooper jumped in combat. My nephew went on to participate in 33 jumps in Korea until 1954 when he returned to the United States. My nephew died June 2016 in Huntington, WV. The US army was segregated until integrated by President Harry S. Truman after World War II in 1945.

Jim Crow laws have almost faded out of our US Services. Orientation classes in the service are given and barriers have opened up to create a healthy, wholesome atmosphere of understanding between blacks and whites.

Military service remained important to the Howard and Harper families. Here Doris's son Robert Lee Harper is leaving for the United States Army from Huntington Airport in 1971.

Chapter 7
Church Life

Sunday Mornings in the Family

My Aunt Minnie (my mother's sister) and Uncle Henry Stuart lived across Kelley's Field, which was behind my parents' home on Effinger Street.[2] Some weekends I spent at their house on Johnson Street. Mother and Aunt Minnie were great cooks, and Sunday morning each prepared a big breakfast in their home. It was not out of the ordinary for the menu to be:

1) fried fish (caught from the river), fried potatoes, eggs, oatmeal, coffee, milk, juice, biscuits; or,
2) sausage, fried apples, eggs, oats, beverages, biscuits or hot rolls; or,
3) country ham, eggs, fried potatoes, oats, always biscuits or hoecake bread baked with plenty of jam, jelly, apple butter.

Before we come to the table to eat, we all gathered in the parlor (living room) for prayer on our knees. Aunt would always say, "Now Daddy, don't pray too long—the food will get cold," and even when we sat down to the kitchen table she would say the same thing because "Unca" would go on and on.

After breakfast before 9:30 on Sunday morning we walked a block or so to church on Kelley Street. Our church, Bethel African Methodist Episcopal (established in 1893) was dedicated to the community as well as two other churches, John Wesley Methodist Church and First Baptist Church. At Bethel AME, my Aunt Minnie and Uncle Henry belonged there and did the maintenance,

---

[2] Henry (b. 1893) & Minnie (b. 1894) Stuart owned their two-story frame house at 629 N. Broad St. where they lived with their children Henry, Jr. (b. 1916) and Norma (b. 1920). Henry was the head cook at Harrisonburg's prestigious Kavanaugh Hotel.

were in charge of administrative affairs at the church and kept everything functioning. They fed the preacher every Sunday although he lived in the parsonage owned by the church. Bethel was a busy, happy little church, full all day on Sunday and Wednesday nights. Whether people joined church or not, they were forever coming to get the Holy Ghost, shouting and rejoicing and praising the Lord. We children liked to see the celebration. We never poked fun, just quietly took it all in.

Bethel AME Church at 184 Kelley St.

Everyone Went to Church

Sunday was a day of praise and thanksgiving to all Newtown residents. Not only did all families give table blessings but also, like our family, they went to church and really praised the Lord. Our three black churches were instrumental not only in preaching the word of God, but they also had a strong impact on the Newtown families, each having their own denomination, yet always working together in unison in a crisis whether major or minor. Church was an essential meeting place for brothers, sisters, and cousins. It was our source of information, our day in court, our togetherness, our happy/sad hours, our family hours, and our fellowship. It was where we had conferences, conventions, weddings, and funerals, prayed, made decisions, and solved domestic problems, church or worldly. Residents, however, talked about politics very little or mostly not at all around children. This was done privately in the homes or at the Colonnade Hall for adults only.

The original John Wesley Methodist Episcopal Church (founded in 1865) on Liberty Street. This structure was torn down in the 1950s and the church rebuilt at 445 Sterling Street in Newtown.

    Church was fully attended regardless of denomination. Everybody knew each other. Children were taught to listen and be attentive. All churches including Broad Street Mennonite Church had three services on Sunday and prayer meeting on Wednesday. Each church had its own church bell to ring at a designated time, never mixing up. Sunday church always began with Sunday school at 9:30A.M., then church at 11A.M., and evening worship at 7:30P.M. Our three churches rang those bells in all their glory to call people together. I well remember when the first bell rang, my sisters and I would make conversation like:

"Which bell was that?"

"The first one."

"Oh yes, that is correct."

John Wesley Methodist Episcopal Church (now United Methodist), located on Liberty Street, sold their property to Wetsel Seed Company and moved to Sterling and Effinger Streets. There they built a new church in 1939. As a child of four years old, I was christened in this church and attended Sunday School regularly. As an adult, I taught Sunday School at this church for twenty-two years, was youth council president for twelve, took my three children, my nieces, nephews, half the neighborhood (as many as a dozen) every Sunday to Sunday School.

First Baptist Church on Wolfe Street, established in 1878, was our largest church at the time. Perhaps fifty families owned homes around it. Later it was sold to redevelopment and demolished. Then the church bought property on Broad Street and Kelley Street and very soon after that (in 1964), a new church was built.

First Baptist Church (built in 1878) was at the corner of E. Wolfe St. and Mason St. Destroyed by the Urban Renewal Program, a new church was built at 611 Broad St.

Gay Street Mennonite Mission moved to Broad Street and renamed their church, which was owned and operated by their congregation. The property was once an apple orchard with about a dozen trees and one cherry tree. There were three families (Webb, Brocks, and Curry) during my childhood that joined the Broad Street Mennonite Church. Each was dedicated to the church and stayed until the children grew up through high school.

Revival meetings were held in tents in big fields. They were part of a movement called "religious awakening." There would be singing, preaching, and testifying sometimes way into the night. Adults would sing and dance and shout 'til they got the Holy Ghost, so they tell us.

The revival meant so much to our elders. We could tell because they expressed themselves; they were happy and full of laughter. We watched and kept quiet as we were taught to do, and some of us would fall asleep. When church was over, we were taken home and everybody went to bed. Next day, we were busy getting all chores done for the big camp meeting that again was going to be. Usually it was held for a week. Each church had a chance to have its own.

After church on Sunday was ball time: tennis, basketball, baseball, and weather permitting, we were all out. Curfew for the entire city was at 9 P.M. Police walked their beats and were recognized for their friendliness and respect to all. They did not walk beats in any other part of the city, only in Newtown.

Gay Street Mennonite Mission (c. 1940).
Image courtesy of Eastern Mennonite University Historical Library.

My fond memory of Mennonites has strong roots in my early life. I was eight years old when I first attended the Gay Street Mission before they moved. The Mission was one block off N. Main Street coming up Gay Street. It was a one-story building with one huge room. It moved from Gay Street and Federal Alley to Broad Street and the corner of Effinger and was renamed Broad Street Mennonite Church.

As I remember in the 1930s and 1940s, I was taught at a very early age the Old and New Testament at their church. It was an interesting way of learning the Bible. We were told it in stories, and it seemed so much easier to remember. Then we recited what we read and before you knew it, you were remembering all about the book.

After attending our church, we were free to go to the Mennonites' church. The mission service was not the same time as our church service. On the roof hung a great big bell, and Sunday morning our superintendent, Ernest Swartzentruber, rang it loud and proud greeting everyone. They had Sunday School, then morning service, and later another service at 7:30 P.M. every Sunday. Our neighborhood was popular with children. Some did not have a church home so they filled the Gay Street Mission half full before the others got out of their churches.

For many years Doris attended the Gay Street Mission Bible School. In this 1941 photo she is in the back just to the left of the open door. Image courtesy of Eastern Mennonite University Historical Library.

Ernest L. Swartzentruber was the Bible School superintendent. Theirs was not the same time ours was. In fact, the Mission always checked with our churches and then they decided on their date. Each year, one black Mennonite lady from Lancaster, Pennsylvania, came down to teach Bible School.[3] We welcomed and enjoyed having her. There was always a yearly picture taken of our group, and in 1939 we had sixty in attendance. We thought that was a big year. Integration had not been enforced at that time so we were an all black congregation. Except for the lady from Pennsylvania, our teachers were all white and lived in Park View, north of the city.

Often in the summer, well before 1940, we would hike to Park View (which we called Mennonite Town) and have a picnic with any family the teachers set it up with. From Gay Street, we walked up over what was then called Deep Pole Hill (Liberty Street), turned left at the livestock market, now Kratzer Road, on through to Route 42 (called Virginia Avenue now), straight ahead to the wide-open spaces or a farm on the left. We sang songs from our Bible School. My favorite was "The B-i-b-l-e, yes, that's the book for me, I know it is, I'm sure it is, the B-i-b-l-e." I never heard it any more in my lifetime, but I never forgot it. We played games; we had plenty of peanut butter and jelly sandwiches, fresh berries, homemade cookies, and plenty of lemonade and sometimes milk. Our closing program at the mission Bible school was always a program at night that parents looked forward to. We recited by memory Bible verses and Bible stories, as well as characters in the Bible along with the names of all the disciples. That was a special night. All this happened at the Gay Street

---

[3] This woman was Rowena Lark, an African-American woman who joined the Mennonite church in Pennsylvania in 1927; in 1946 her husband, James, became the first African American ordained in the Mennonite church. Rowena helped with the Gay Street Mission's bible school first in 1936 and continued to participate for a number of years thereafter. For full details on the Gay Street Mission see chapter two "Prayer-Covered Protest," in Tobin Miller Shearer's *Daily Demonstrators: The Civil Rights Movement in Mennonite Homes and Sanctuaries* (Baltimore: Johns Hopkins University Press, 2010).

Mission. In later years, when it moved to Broad Street, the congregation was not as large, but the church still carried on. Mennonites were a warm cheerful group of people and today, eight decades later, I find my roots again in a retirement community owned and under the direction of the Mennonite Churches.

Immanuel Mennonite Church on Kelley Street in recent years is very active, and both black and white attend. It also has a child care center open daily. They have come in joyfully and full of the spirit of the Lord. We are pleased to have their presence. They have shown dignity and poise to our people, and we feel we are one in the spirit.

Some people may still remember Elder Darcus, who was a popular preacher in the Northeast of Harrisonburg for a time. From 1952 to 1978, Elder Henry C. Darcus started three churches in the Harrisonburg area. The Stuarts Draft native started preaching when he was a deacon in a Staunton Church. The pastor heard of his preaching and told him, "stop running around, I'll give you a chance to preach." After two years of preaching in Staunton, Darcus met a Shenandoah Virginia man named Sam Cubbage, who invited him to come preach in his home. Darcus said he stood in the corner of the Cubbage home and preached to a packed house. Since it looked clear to say they needed a larger meeting house, Darcus rented an empty building on 50 E. Gay Street in Harrisonburg, fixed it up and started The House of Deliverance Church of God and Christ. Four years later they were over-crowding and built a church on Effinger Street off of Broad, where he added an apartment for his family.

Elder Darcus was married and, at the time they lived in Harrisonburg, had four daughters: Sheary, Alecia, Cynthia, and Vernice. Their mother started teaching them to sing when they were at a very early age. They harmonized well and sang all over the Valley. Their singing at the church brought such a large crowd often there had to be police directing traffic around the church-goers. Later, four more children arrived in the family.

The House of Deliverance Church of God and Christ

Elder Darcus also helped start the Highway of Holiness Church in Luray, Virginia, but after twenty years it was turned over to another congregation because Elder Darcus's schedule was too hectic to continue serving. He felt honored and pleased to have had four members at The House of Deliverance in Harrisonburg become ministers of the gospel.

When Elder Darcus retired from Dupont in Waynesboro, Virginia, he left his churches, The House of Deliverance of God and Christ in Harrisonburg, and Friendship Church in Staunton, Virginia to move to Norfolk, Virginia to be Associate Minister and Sunday School Superintendent to the bishop at the Church of God and Christ for the denomination's sixty-two churches in Virginia.

Elder Darcus called Harrisonburg his launching pad, and though he moved to Norfolk, Virginia he always came back to visit. His daughter Sheary was the first African-American to graduate from Madison College, in Harrisonburg.[4] Later, Vernice graduated also. Elder Darcus passed away several years ago and left a brother Phillip in the ministry in Charlottesville, Virginia, and his brother Archie, a traveling evangelist.

Sunday Lawn Parties

One exciting event that the whole community would take part in was church lawn parties. Lawn parties were held throughout the summer as a way to fundraise for the churches. They were always announced by word of mouth. Each church took turns at their time to have the lawn party on their lawn, beginning around 5 P.M. Then they would string a roll of lights and go until about 10 P.M. or maybe 11 P.M. Always number one was homemade ice cream, sold by the dish, and then there was fried chicken placed in wash tubs covered with a tablecloth, pies and cakes, cookies, and country ham sandwiches were a fast seller. Food was always sold out for all the food was homemade and people knew it. There would be quartet singers to fill the evening. People sat around and children played on the church ground.

More Fundraisers

Our three black churches in Newtown were very busy with programs to make money for the church. Each church sent announcements to the other two churches on what they were doing for their program and when it would take place. Then the next time the other would plan first; they exchanged like that, and it ran smoothly.

---

[4] In 1964, Sheary Darcus Johnson and a few other local black students were the first to desegregate Harrisonburg High School, and then upon graduation, she became one of the first black students at Madison College (now James Madison University) and the first black graduate in 1970. She later also earned an MA in Library Science from JMU as well. See Janet Smith's "'It was Meant to Be': Madison's first African American Graduate earned her degree 50 years ago" in *James Madison University News* [online] (April 29, 2020): www.jmu.edu/news/2020/04/29-mm-it-was-meant-to-be-sheary-darcus-johnson.shtml.

Besides the Newtown Lawn Parties that we call Bake Sales today, there were Mock Weddings, Tom Thumb Weddings, and Pageants where pupils from school were taught to recite poetry, to sing, carry the right tune, or to act as in the movies. There were Fashion Shows with all ages, always one in the spring and then again in the fall, and Talent Shows with all ages as well as the community where older persons participated. Dancing in the Church was also allowed. The community did not use the school for public activities.

Several ladies had sewing machines and costumes were easily made. There were lots of pretty prints from the Mill feed bags for 25¢ a bag. Women made all kinds of articles and costumes from them.

The best feeling of all was when you presented a program and the church was filled. When First Baptist or AME presented their program, everybody went. It was a family community and everybody went. Coming together taught our children togetherness.

Christmas was the most decorated time of the year. Never did the churches compete. They just decorated and came up with different displays. Each church had a Christmas play. Even though the story may have been told before, the churches worked hard to make theirs the best.

Then on Christmas, like Thanksgiving, there would be family dinners, but only at Thanksgiving would there be wild game and turkey that the fathers had caught while hunting. We had so many different species of animals such as deer, birds, rabbit, squirrel, and bear.

Church doors were never locked, and churches were always lit up at night whether there were services or fundraisers or not. In the winter you could always go inside to get warm. The pot belly stove was fed Red Ash or Pocahontas coal through the day and night.[5] No one took advantage of the church, and there was no marking up or vandalism. People brought burlap sacks of coal to church and arms of chopped wood. Meetings of all sorts

---

[5] The Red Ash and Pocahontas coal mines in Virginia & West Virginia provided Harrisonburg with most of its coal.

concerning the Newtown Community met regularly at the church. That was another reason the fires burned day and night. Whatever your church took up in offering for these events belonged to your congregation, and today that would be called a Fundraiser.

Taking Care of the Dead

Funerals were held at the church, at residences, and at graveside. At residences, the immediate family, as many as could be, were inside, others on the porch outside or on the sidewalk. Bodies were not embalmed those days and quick to burial they went. We had a well- known funeral parlor owned by the Updike family.

I watched my mother scrub and wash my 87-year-old grandmother, whom the Doctor had come by and pronounced dead. Then she was dressed and moved to our parlor (living room) where she lay for two days; then the undertaker (as we called them) came and took her to the funeral parlor to be laid in a casket the family had picked out. Third day they brought her body back and stayed out front of the house until our short service was held and then on to the cemetery. Some rode in the few cars, but most walked.

Our cemetery was three blocks away and within walking distance, so all but the immediate family walked.[6] The cemetery was well kept by family members, and it looked like a garden. The people in the Newtown community took great pride in protecting and constantly cleaning up. There was no trash or vandalism, no custodian. Family and friends were caretakers. Everyone knew everyone.

Memorial Day was a special day with families coming from faraway places to communicate with loved ones. The older part of the cemetery was like sacred grounds—no playing, no trespassing, and lots of respect for the deceased. We were taught these are your saints; they have gone home.

---

[6] The land for Newtown Cemetery was purchased in 1868 for burial of local African Americans. This is the only black cemetery in Harrisonburg. In December 2014, the cemetery was entered on the Virginia Landmarks Register.

Complicated Passings

My first cousin lived in New York City. She was my godmother, and when she passed away in 1970, I had to take her parents and my aunt and uncle to her funeral. Neither they nor I had ever been to the "Big Apple" as it was called. I had no map. A friend gave me directions like go north on Route 11 to the Pennsylvania Turnpike, get on, go to Scranton, Pennsylvania and get off when you see the exit for New York City. It should be 34th Street. Go up 34th to 154th and I was at my destination. We arrived on Tuesday morning.

Tuesday night, May 26, we received a call from home in Virginia that my father had died of a heart attack. So, early on the 26th I drove back to Virginia. The funeral was planned for Thursday of that week. After my father's funeral, I left Virginia early Friday to go back to New York for the funeral services on Saturday for my godmother.

On Monday morning, I started back with my aunt and uncle to Virginia as their daughter was being transported by train for burial in Newtown. As we were leaving New York, we had only gotten to the outskirts when we had a flat tire. I had two seniors in their seventies in a car without an air conditioner on a hot day in June. Fortunately, I was able to guide the car over to the curb, and to my surprise, I was across from a garage. There, I purchased a tire for $35. After they mounted and put it on, we were off again toward Virginia.

We arrived on Tuesday and the body came by train on Thursday. The funeral was held the same day. Her parents, my aunt and uncle, and I made a safe trip back to Virginia, and all was well.

Chapter 8
SCHOOL DAYS

This photo shows Broad Street Mennonite Church, with Effinger School in the background. Peggy Curry and daughter Naomi are walking on the sidewalk. The Howards' car is also in the foreground. The Urban Renewal Program razed the school and today, Rose's and other businesses occupy the School's site and the lower part of Effinger street seen here.

I attended the Effinger Street School (four rooms built in 1882 with three rooms added in 1910) located on East Effinger Street. One-fourth of the half basement was a restroom for girls and one-fourth was a restroom for boys, plus a furnace room. Both restrooms had outside entrances. The huge furnace ran nonstop twenty-four hours a day in winter. Mr. Martin, our janitor, lived across the street with his family.

All classes were taught under the same roof and had the same entrance. There was no cafeteria at Effinger. Students brought either baggie lunches or went home if they lived close, as long as you returned before the bell rang. If you were tardy, you got detention and no one wanted that. Classrooms on the second floor were sometimes used for gym. Two classrooms on the second floor were also used at times for assembly and home economics. Also on the second floor was a very small room for the principal's office.

Several large trees bordered the school grounds, with several acres around. Also closely surrounding the building were bushes that bloomed all white every spring. A grassy front yard made a very attractive setting.

Lucy F. Simms at the Effinger Street School in 1930.

Row 1 left to right: Austin Dickerson, unknown, Red Bundy, Elon Rhodes, Norman Harris, unknown, unknown, ? Madden, unknown, Joe Yokley
Row 2 left to right: Unknown, Elsie Scott, Ralph Sampson, next three unknown, BoBo Sampson, unknown, Wilmer Byrd, unknown, Moe Thomas
Row 3 left to right: Anna Frances Edmonson, Roberta Wells, unknown, Louise Winston (last to be deceased in February 2019), unknown, Sam Margaret Carter, unknown, Lillian Scott, Marseline Ray, Esther Sampson, Ann Howard

This was my school. All classes were taught under the same roof and same entrance. It was also the school at which Ms. Lucy F. Simms taught. She graduated from Hampton University in 1877 and was a student there at the same time as Booker T. Washington. She taught in our Newtown Community for 55 years, until she passed away in 1934. I was in her classes as a young child. My two sisters and three brothers also all attended the Effinger Street School.

We always were taught the value of Black History and self-expression, even though we lived under Jim Crow laws. Below is our school newspaper, *The Chatterbox*, of Thursday, February 28th, 1935. The newspaper was published monthly by the Effinger Street School Student Publication Board. All of our black students made up the staff.

The Effinger High School student publication, *Chatterbox*, was published monthly. My cousin Naomi Stuart and brother-in-law Rawley Bundy were contributors. Mr. Bundy was my brother in-law Red Bundy's brother, who was married to my sister Julia Howard.

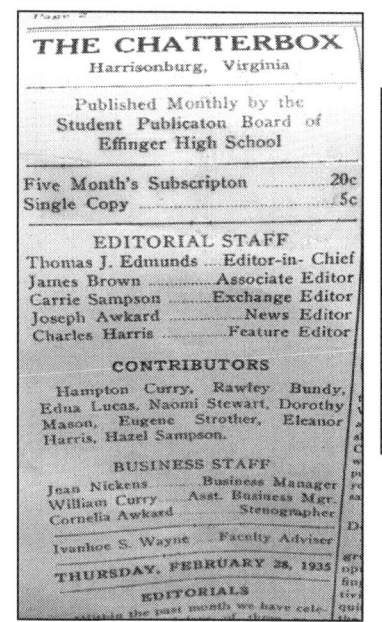

Images of The Chatterbox courtesy of Duffy Smith

The "Dear Editor" section of *The Chatterbox* was written by my first cousin Naomi Stuart. As you can see, she was an intellectual student that focused on what was then called Negro History. We learned the value early of Black History that came from our ancestors. Her mother, Minnie Stuart, was my mother Julia Howard's sister and David Stuart's grandmother. We all lived in our Newtown community of northeast Harrisonburg, VA.

There was an article about the Effinger Street school honor roll in the student *Chatterbox* school newsletter, and here was my name when I was in the first grade, "Doris Jean Howard," a proud student of Ms. Lucy F. Simms.

> **HONOR ROLL SHOWS UP-WARD SCHOLASTIC TREND**
>
> The Honor Roll for the first Semester released from the principal's office this week shows a remarkable increase in better than average work as compared with the work done within the same period during the 1933-34 session.
>
> In compiling the honor roll the following points are used as determinents: attendance, scholarship, conduct and general cooperation. The following Honor Roll includes both the elementary and high school.
>
> First Grade—Lester Carter, James Curry, Robert ruce Goodlowe, Arnold Howard, Carlton Woody, Lindbergh Yoakeley, Calvin Hill, Mildred Burgess, Julia Buck, Nannie Franklin, Peggy Harris, Margaret Harris, Maxine Holly, Doris Jean Howard, Thelma Madden, Emily Mosby, Lucille Watson, Mary Watson, Mary Lewis, Bernice Sampson.
>
> Second Grade—George Buck, Neil Holly, Johnny Morris, Mary Woody.
>
> Third Grade—Ruth Jones, Sheldon Smith, Emily Stevens, Roland Temple, Ella Mae Turner, Robert Tolliver.
>
> Fourth Grade—Edna Tolliver, Lois Rauser, Eris Washington, Mary Wil-

The Effinger Street school honor roll in The Chatterbox, the school newsletter of 1933-34. Note the mention of first-grader "Doris Jean Howard," a proud student of Ms. Lucy F. Simms during her last year of teaching —she died in July of 1934.

Our school never had all new books. We may have gotten a few, but not for everybody. We called them leftovers or hand me downs. You could see they were used because they were torn or soiled. The parents never complained. I often wondered what would have happened if they had done so. Our school, until later years, did not have a PTA. Parents and teachers complained and did planning among themselves. The superintendent (who was white) seldom visited our school, and when he did, he was in and out. No other whites ever came. We had all colored teachers.

120

Mary Awkard Fairfax, Second grade teacher at Lucy F. Simms School in 1960. She was a Columbia University Teachers College graduate. Doris's daughter Belinda is the tall girl in the back right with a black sweater.

    Segregation was in high gear. No sports were played together, and there was no communication in any way between black and white students. Segregation prohibited the association of blacks and whites' period—no explanation. In fact, I never entered their school all my school life. Our school used the cast-off white school uniforms and choir robes while their school purchased new ones. They were generally in good shape, however.

    In my younger days, like ten or twelve years old, we talked among ourselves wondering why we couldn't have a bigger school, better school. We would not have to have two or three grades in one classroom, like Ms. Lucy had in her beginner's class. There was no such thing as kindergarten; she had first and some second graders. Ms. Hollins had some second and third, maybe fourth graders. Ms. Davies had two classes. When they rolled over, all the grades were crowded. I remember we had forty-five in our fifth grade. We played at wishing we had a big school and wondered if we would ever have one.

Between 1901-1902 Virginia rewrote its constitution, openly acknowledging that their goal was to disenfranchise African-Americans in a way that would not technically violate the 14th and 15th amendments that specifically gave black people the right to vote. Though it took over a year, in the end, they accomplished this goal, eliminating the vote for African-Americans (and many poor whites), and also firmly establishing segregation laws that kept blacks and whites separated in schools, and in all civic and social venues, well into the 1960s.

School Sports

At the Effinger School an alley (now Community Street) bordered on one end of the grounds, and on that end of the school grounds was our tennis court used daily. The court was also used for basketball. It was constantly in use, even when school was not in session. There was always play for either sport. The ground was smooth and hard (no cement), and it stayed like that year after year.

On the back side of the school was a football field. PE, or physical education, was practiced there as it was a priority, and all classes were assigned to it as long as the weather permitted. We didn't have any bleachers. We stood for all games.

On the right side of the building was a softball diamond, also used for baseball. We had numerous teams among ourselves, and baseball was a favorite.

Children's games, beside baseball, were jumping ropes, marbles, hop scotch, hide and go seek, Little Sally Walker, Farmer in the Dell, and so on. These games went on daily over and over. There was tennis and track for the older children, mostly in spring. The spring was a fun time for all on the playground. Teams were measuring up for the competition between schools that they faced before the school year closed. Every school had a field day in May. Everybody wanted to win so lots of practice had to be done. This was something to look forward to. Field day had all kinds of races and games and lasted all day. Food was sold or served also. It was a fun day for all.

Basketball

We usually practiced basketball on the tennis court at Effinger, but when the weather was bad, we went to a building called The Colonnade, four blocks from our school. We did not have a gym; therefore, we played all our competitive games of basketball at the Colonnade through a rental agreement between the School Board and our school. Integration had not been accomplished yet so we played all black schools. The Colonnade also hosted many other events. Name bands from all over came to play. They got famous later: Count Basie, Duke Ellington, Jimmy Dorsey, too many to remember.

Neither Effinger Street School nor any other black school owned or had access to a school bus. We rode in private family cars to our prospective games that were out of town. Concerned citizens in the community also acted as chaperones. The team never spent nights away. Regardless of late games, we always returned home.

Each School was in charge of ticket sales at the door as it paid for their team expense. Tickets were fifty cents at each school. The School provided a meal for the team. We played all six schools during our scheduled year back-to-back—that made twelve games; then March was the tournament. Whoever won, received the trophy. Girls played first at each game so we had a double game.

The newly completed Lucy F. Simms School opened its doors in 1939.

Lucy F. Simms School and More Basketball

The Effinger Street School closed in 1939, the same year we moved to our new school, Lucy Simms. The new school had an inside gymnasium/auditorium, showers, cafeteria, Industrial Arts Dept., Home Economics Dept., and restrooms with running water. We had never before practiced on such a beautiful hardwood floor.

Our team was so proud of our new school we got busy practicing, and in 1943 we beat Booker T. Washington of Staunton, Addison of Roanoke, Dunbar of Lynchburg, Roosevelt of Waynesboro, Carver of Salem, and Thomas Jefferson of Charlottesville, Virginia, all colored schools. Our coaches were Albert Edwards and Elaine Bryant.

Male trainers are D. Vickers and E. Johnson; women in the middle: Doris Howard, Eddie Harris, Maxine Holley; top: Mary Williams and Delores Davis. (Absent are Julia Howard, Ruth Jones, and Beulah Walker.)

After beating all those other schools, the girls' basketball teacher, Elaine Bryant, took us to the big championship playoff. Our final win over St. Francis Catholic School for Girls on the outskirts of Richmond, Virginia allowed us to come home with the bacon. All of the team members (pictured below) include my sister Julia Howard, Mary Williams, Ruth Jones, Beulah Walker, Eddie Harris, Maxine Holley, Delores Davis, and myself, Doris Howard.

1943 Lucy F. Simms School Women's Basketball Team

Doris's Son Billo Harper (10 years old) was team manager of Lucy F. Simms Bulldogs Basketball Team twenty years later in 1963.

The Ebony Players

In front: Charlotte Williams Taylor and Doris Howard; standing from left to right: Loretta Price, Geraldine Spinerd, Susie Bryant, Wilhelmina Tutt, Bernice Tolliver, and Dorothy Burgess.

The Ebony Players at Lucy Simms School was organized, produced, and directed by Theodore (Buddy) Tolliver in 1940, a fellow eighth-grade student who was younger than all the girls in the picture. Girls present were Loretta Price, Wilhelmina Tutt, Bernice Tolliver, Dorothy Burgess, Doris Howard, Susie Bryant, Charlotte Williams, and Geraldine Spinerd. Our Home Economic Department made the costumes, which included white aprons, red bandanas and black T-shirts with black leotards. The Ebony Player sign was painted Red.

Buddy created the musical skits from the production of the Ziegfeld Follies that came out in 1907. Then the movie was later shown, and he copied all he could gather. The original Ziegfeld

Follies were a series of elaborate theatrical productions on Broadway in New York City from 1907-31.

The Ziegfeld movie was a true all-star extravaganza featuring the likes of some of our most popular movie stars, such as Judy Garland, Esther Williams, Lena Horne, Fred Astaire, Gene Kelly, Red Skelton, and Lucille Ball, in a series of musical numbers and comedy sketches like you would see in the Ziegfeld Follies. We practiced in our school gym, on the school playground, at home in our back yards—we were dancing everywhere. Soon it was show time, and we were ready. The school had a program, and we were asked to appear—no problem—we were ready. A success it was, and we played again and again throughout the year; in fact, we were together for two school terms.

The "N" Word

The "N" word was seldom used in school (unless in a whisper) or in fighting or fussing. Sometimes it was used in a figure of speech like: "Lord, these 'N' and poor white trash." My brother came home one day crying and told my mother a white boy hit him with a rock. She asked, "What did you do to him?" He said, "He called me the 'N' word, and I called him dirty white trash." Mother said, "Stop crying, you broke even."

There are so many stories about the "N" word, like the one about my aunt who gave us kids a hard time. One day we had a big game of marbles going when here she comes to the door. "You little pickaninny 'Ns!' Get them marbles outta my flower bed!" See, I was a tomboy and played with the boys.

We did not use the "N" word at school or church. That was a big no-no. You would get your mouth washed out with soap at either place by any grown up. Older siblings used it more loosely anytime among themselves, especially in fighting, but we younger ones were not among their friends. Our ages separated us. We knew our place in our age group.

Teachers

We had all black teachers who stayed on the job a long time and were mostly singles. Our kindergarten/first grade teacher was Miss Lucy F. Simms who taught me six months or more before her death.

In the 1960s Doris was heavily involved with the PTA of the Simms school. Here she is with the much-loved and respected long-time principal of both the Effinger and Simms schools, W. N. P. Harris.

The new school was named after her, the Lucy F. Simms School. After her death, Miss Jeanne Francis took her place. Other teachers were Miss Ruth Hollins, Miss Anna Marie Snyder, Miss Dorothy Davies, Miss Rhoda Ross, Miss Walker, Miss Elaine Bryant, Coach Edwards, Mr. McCain, and Mr. Wayne, a music instructor.

There was no bullying ever. Teachers were in close contact with students at all times. The ruler or yard stick was frequently used with parent approval. The coatroom was always open for spanking/whipping.

Lucy F. Simms School Classmates, Doris Howard, Nancy Fields, Eddie Harris, and Wanetta Curry

Our teachers were at school from 8 A.M. to 4 P.M.; then they walked home (none had cars). They stopped for parent visitation if necessary since most mothers did not work, and they were always at home. In the 1930s, few blacks had cars. People walked everywhere, not hurriedly, just a natural walk. There were two cabs in the entire city: Rai's, a black taxi 25¢, and Robinson's, a white taxi that cost 50¢ round trip.

Our principal did not drive or own a car. He, like all the teachers, walked. He lived on Johnson Street, four blocks from Effinger Street School. Miss Lucy Simms, for whom the new school was named, also lived four blocks away on Johnson Street. In fact, they were neighbors. Both owned their properties. Here I shall describe more about the teachers at Effinger Street and Lucy F. Simms Schools from 1939 to 1945.

Miss Lucy F. Simms, first grade teacher, first taught at Longs Chapel in the late-1800s at Zenda outside of Harrisonburg, about six miles away.

Longs Chapel in Zenda was built in the 1870s but was abandoned in the 1920s and fell into disrepair.

Doris Harper Allen at Longs Chapel at Zenda in the 2010s after it was restored by Al Jenkins with assistance from local community organizations.

She was a very fine black lady, quick to use the yard stick, and in those days permission was granted by parents. Miss Lucy became ill suddenly and left school after teaching for fifty-six years. Her passing brought the last group of people together that were associated with the school. Her property was donated to the Board of Education for a new school for black children in the northeast of the city (Newtown).

Miss Jean Francis, a native of Harrisonburg, graduated from Virginia State College in Petersburg, Virginia. She lived with her parents, three blocks from school, and was selected to fill the shoes of the deceased Miss Simms. Miss Jean had her little ones daily in Phys. Ed. classes with "A" grade mark requirement from the Board of Education. All classes were in accord with the white school throughout the school. Miss Jean followed the school to Simms and continued to teach PE.

Miss Ruth Hollins, a native of Harrisonburg, also graduated from Virginia State College in Petersburg. She lived with her family, about five blocks from the school and walked to school every day. Miss Hollins was more firm than any other teacher in Effinger. She kept order in her class as well as any other if she needed to. She taught second and third grades and had no trouble with discipline. A P.T.A. formed and all of the parents attended and gave one hundred percent permission to the teachers to correct students in any way, and then you also got spanked when you got home. Miss Ruth moved to the Simms School and taught third grade there.

Miss Dorothy Davies, a native of Roanoke, Virginia, was also a graduate of Virginia State College. She lived with the Mosby family here in the city. Miss Davies taught fourth grade. She was a very dedicated woman who believed everyone could learn and do well. There was the ruler for those who were lazy and thought otherwise. Everyone passed her class. They were glad to get out and pass to another room.

Miss Snyder, a native of Salem, Virginia, came by bus to teach at Effinger Street School. She did not drive or own a car, the same as the other teachers. Miss Snyder, too, graduated from Virginia State College in Petersburg, Virginia, and lived with the Mosbys on Johnson Street. She was very quiet, a unique young lady but very firm in getting the message across. She taught fifth and sixth grades and moved on to the Lucy Simms School.

Miss Walker came from Richmond, Virginia. She taught home economics (we called it home making) in one big room on the second floor at Effinger Street School. The sixth graders were the first ones given Home Ec. classes in sewing, cooking, table setting, making menus, housekeeping, and etiquette. Boys in sixth grade started industrial arts and crafts. Miss Walker left at the end of the school year in 1938.

When we arrived at the Lucy F. Simms School in 1939, we had a new home economics teacher, Miss Morris, from Suffolk, Virginia. The new school had so much space, including a cafeteria. There was a three-room apartment for Home Ec. with a bathroom and kitchen. We continued our studies in cooking, cleaning, sewing, socializing. We even had a beauty parlor. Miss Morris seemed to know so much and taught us so many things to learn quickly. We were kept busy making things like aprons, broomstick skirts, and dresses from cotton feedbags. We all had to have designed and made a complete outfit and be ready to model it in the fashion show at the end of the year.

Miss Elaine Bryant from Staunton, Virginia, was our first female teacher in physical education. She began her tenure at Simms school in 1939. She coached the girls' basketball team and took them on to win a championship game in 1944.

Miss Oliver, a native of Petersburg and a graduate of the Virginia State College, taught English at Simms from 1939 to 1955. She was fluent in three other languages and taught all the English classes in grades 8, 9, 10, 11, and 12. She lived in an apartment on Broad Street and walked the six blocks to school daily but rode the bus when going home at the close of school. Those were the days we sat in the rear of the bus.

Mr. Edwards, a native of Norfolk, Virginia, came to Effinger Street School and then to Simms. He coached boys and girls and taught physical education. I repeat, P.E. was top priority. We had it all through school from elementary on up. Mr. Edwards taught basketball, tennis, and volleyball to all classes. He also taught algebra and geometry. As coach, he was excited to move to Simms from Effinger Street School since there was no gym at Effinger. Simms had a beautiful complete gym with hardwood floors and perfectly new baskets.

Mr. McCain, native of Richmond, Virginia, was the mathematics and industrial arts teacher. The new school had a large area in the basement with machinery and equipment for grades eight through twelve. Furniture was made by the students and presented at the school closing. Then it was theirs to take home. Mr. McCain worked hard, making sure each student completed his assignment to get a passing grade. At the end of the year, his efforts were justified. All the students came through because they knew the pieces were theirs to take home.

Winter and School

When it snowed, the ground would be covered over and over 'til we got about fourteen to eighteen inches. We did lots of sleigh riding. The parents always shoveled the snow so the kids could get to school. I remember the men on Effinger Street made tunnels or paths to school from my house, across the street, and to the school house because it was warmer at school than it was in our homes. We could go early to school and stay all day. There were no cars or street cleaners, so a path to school was no problem. We never heard such a statement as "no school today." There was always school.

In the basement of the Effinger Street School, on the boys' side of the restroom, was a huge furnace that burned red ash coal that they kept going strong in the cold days of winter. The janitor lived across the street with his family and when Effinger Street School closed, he went on up to Simms School as janitor.

Spring Graduation

Memorial Day weekend always was the proper time set for our school graduation. Baccalaureate was held the same day we honored our deceased at the cemetery. The whole community attended the celebration, young and old. The program was held at the grave of Miss Lucy Simms, our former teacher for whom our school was named. There was a speaker, singing, prayers, more speeches, and loads of flowers. We would march over to Simms at 4 P.M. for the occasion. Out of town families would participate, as well as all the community churches.

Doris Howard (Harper Allen), high school graduate in 1945. Picture taken on Effinger Street, up from her home.

Chapter 9
WORK, JOBS, & THE BACK DOOR

Working After High School

In the mid-1940s, I turned sixteen. You could get a license to work, so I and about fifteen other friends, boys and girls from our neighborhood, sought employment at the Presbyterian Summer Camp at Massanutten Springs, east of our city of Harrisonburg. Our job titles were cooks, waiters, waitresses, bus boys in training for service in the dining room, and chambermaids. Still others were trained for landscaping and taking care of the lawn.

We roomed and boarded at the job. We had quarters in the basement of this very huge hotel five miles from home, far out into the country. Boys roomed on one side and the girls on the other. Our chaperones and supervisors also stayed in the basement.

We were not allowed on the big front porch which ran across the front of the hotel except at early dawn when we scrubbed and cleaned. We never used the front doors, but always entered through the back door. That was the law of the land. (Some establishments used signs that read *Whites Only* over doors.)

Serving three meals a day was a busy chore. We had large groups of youth or adults at this Christian facility daily, each staying a week at a time. Our dining room (for black staff) was on the long back porch which ran across the entire building. There was a pool for Guests Only through the week, but on Saturday after 6 pm, the hired help could swim. Then the pool was drained later in the night and refilled fresh early on Monday. Those were the rules of the landlord, and they were posted as such.

In the summer of 1944, I was employed at one of our three chicken plants, dressing and preparing chickens for market. Again, all blacks, no whites; we weren't allowed to work together. There were no signs up; you just did not apply if you were white.

Later in 1945, after I graduated from Lucy F. Simms School, several bag factories had opened, and blacks could work. Feedbags were shipped in from up north to be sown and patched. They were fairly clean with maybe a little feed left in them.

Both the chicken plants and the bag factory each had white employers, so *White Only* signs were placed over the restroom door. In some instances, restroom signs showed "White Only" with a fist and pointing thumb. The law was obeyed at all times. It was known there would be punishment if not. Warnings were not given. You went to jail if you disobeyed.

There was no conversing with whites. There would only be one designated employer you could communicate with. That person gave you your check on Friday and took any complaint you may have had. There was only one designated entrance for blacks as well.

My first job after high school, I was working at the Southern Bag company (out of Philadelphia), one of many bag factories in Harrisonburg.[7] It was on Rock Street between Federal and Mason and there we washed, mended, and patched used feed bags, and sold them back to the farmers. My job at the bag factory earned me $30 a week, enough to allow me to get dresses made.

That dress (in the photo) was a doozie. In fact, it was homemade. My mother sewed and also had a white lady who sewed. Actually, they were self-made seamstresses, and we just used the term "she sews." I remember this navy blue taffeta ballerina suit I had mother's friend make. Anyway, I bought the material at J. C. Penny's for 49¢ a yard. I never forgot, it took five yards and had a plaid taffeta petticoat under it (it was called a petticoat if it was with ruffles and colorful. It was called underskirt if it was like a slip). The song "Dance, Ballerina, Dance," by Nat King Cole, had just come out.

---

[7] In her notes, Doris wrote that Ron Elyard said there were probably fifteen or so bag factories when the Griffith company started up in 1953, and today it is the only Harrisonburg bag company still in operation. It is located on Waterman Drive. (interview 11/10/14)

Doris in her homemade "Ballerina" dress inspired by the song, "Dance, Ballerina, Dance" first released in 1947 by Jimmy Dorsey & His Orchestra and later re-recorded by Nat King Cole in 1957.

When I was 25 or 26, I was hired by President G. Tyler Miller[8] at Madison College. I cooked and served the meals. During my time of employment there, there were two in the family, President Miller and his wife, Mrs. Miller. I planned the meals and went over them with the madam, and together we decided our menu. Both of my parents taught me to cook and were constantly grooming me. There was no phone-calling back and forth as calling was limited. Only necessary calls were made and none on the job. Memory was my best choice (even though Mrs. Miller had plenty of recipe books). Mrs. Miller couldn't cook at all, so it made my chore very easy. Plus, I had an ambitious desire to cook and create new dishes that made the Millers happy. We entertained a lot as there were always guests.

Employment for Blacks

Here in the Shenandoah Valley, in the first half of the twentieth century, there was lots of employment for blacks as maids, cooks, waiters, porters, chauffeurs, and garbage collectors, and the shoe shine stand was always busy. There was no unemployment. Few had a college degree. Our closest black college was 160 miles away in Petersburg, Virginia, outside of our capitol, Richmond, Virginia. That too was segregated. There was no training school for most jobs, none at all. People learned from others who showed them how.

My male cousins were waiters at the Big Meadows hotel on Skyline Drive in the Blue Ridge Mountains of Virginia. They taught each other, and there were lots of young men working there. My aunts and uncles were cooks here in the city. At age twelve I went with my mother to do catering, cooking, serving, and cleaning. I worked after school and half days on Saturdays during that time. The minimum wage was 25¢ for a while, then 35¢, and it was a long time before 50¢ came into effect.[9]

---

[8] President Miller served from 1949-1971.
[9] The federal hourly minimum wage was established as part of the New Deal in 1938 at 25¢. It went up to 30¢ in 1939, to 40¢ in 1945, 75¢ in

Federal Alley, later called Federal Street, had about ten homeowners. There was a Coca Cola bottling company on the corner of Main and Gay Streets, but it did not hire blacks. Then there was a horse stable owned by whites but run by blacks. It was a training school for rich whites and college students. Sundays it was closed, and blacks groomed and cleaned the stable. Then they could ride and get free lessons. We rode up Gay Street to Conrad Avenue, over to Effinger Street past our school, past my house, and then across Broad Street to the open fields, straight ahead to the Newtown Cemetery and on through to the reservoir, which would make three miles. There were no cars so the roads were clear, although people had the right of way so you had to be careful.

Some people's livelihood was peddling. They came in wagons or horse-drawn buggies, or put up stands on the corners, selling vegetables and all kinds of fruit. Milk off a horse-drawn wagon was sold in pints and quarts in glass bottles. The ice wagon had blocks of ice called cakes of ice that sold small for 15¢, medium for 25¢, and large for 50¢. All these peddlers were persons that lived in our community. There were no strangers. Everybody knew each other.

A white husband and wife ran Dove's Grocery Store on Johnson Street and made their residence in the rear of the building. The store had cold cuts of meat, hamburger, steak, liver, sausage, roasts, and most any kind of meat, whatever you wanted. All the groceries had a big meat unit to sell fresh meats. They had other grocery products as well as a regular grocery store. Store hours were 7:00A.M. to 7:00P.M., six days week.

There were no supermarkets during the 1930–1940s. The smaller grocery stores stayed busy and were always stocking up. Imagine going to the store with a quarter to buy a loaf of bread

---

1950, and then to $1 in 1956. However, many of the most common professions for African Americans such as agricultural work and most service jobs, which accounted for one third of black labor, were not covered by minimum wage laws until the 1966 Fair Labor Standards Act guaranteed it for all workers.

that cost 5¢, one pound of hamburger for 11¢ a pound, 4¢ worth of potatoes and then receive 5¢ change. The grocery store in Newtown had one or two giant refrigerator meat coolers in the store, and they carried basic meats and cheese, hamburger (which was very popular), sausage, and lots of pork, some cuts of steak, oysters when in season, meat like country ham, and wild meat when in season. There were no freezers in any of the stores. A grocery store on South Main Street started out small and outgrew its boundary and later moved in town to Main Street. It continued to grow and prosper until by the 1950s–1960s, it had to move again to East Wolfe Street. Soon here come the supermarkets 1, 2, 3. Bye-bye all the little markets.

Loewner's market was owned by a Jewish family and stood on the corner of Court Square and East Market Street. It was one of the markets put out of business by the coming of the supermarket age.[10]

---

[10] Many Harrisonburg businesses were owned by Jewish people at the time. Doris noted that Newtown residents liked working for them because they were generally wealthy and often generous.

Spitzer's Market was on Gay Street, but they lived elsewhere. The father, mother, and two brothers worked the store. There were no supermarkets in the whole city, but it had lots of little markets. There was McLaughlin's on Main and Gay Streets. Whites owned Bee Bees restaurant on Federal Alley in the Newtown area. Mr. Johnson's Tea Room on Gay Street that was family owned by grandparents, mother, sister, and grandson, and Uncle Lennie's ice cream parlor on Wolfe Street. Except for Bee Bees, all of these were black-owned. Miss Jenny's Tea Room on Wolfe Street was black-owned. The Tea Room was run by Miss Jenny and Charles, her husband, who owned their home across the street. Meals were served and drinks were also. There were booths and counter service, and also a jukebox with musical selections of your choice. There was plenty of room to dance and we did.

Mr. Tankins and Mr. Harris owned and operated the only barber shop in town for blacks. Mr. Tankins owned the shop, and he and his wife owned their home as did Mr. Harris. On Wolfe Street is where all the blacks were owners and entrepreneurs.

There were more colored barbers than white in our city of Harrisonburg. They rented shops downtown on Main Street and other main sections of the business area. These were shops for white customers only. Oscar and Babe Tankins were brothers who rented a shop along the side of Fletcher's Drug store facing Main Street. The drug store faced Court Square. Other barbers were Elon Rhodes, Charlie Nickens, and Charlie Venny. As barbers advanced, they moved out and opened their own shops for whites only. We all remembered Jesse Turner who was one of the early barbers who serviced only white clientele.

In all barbershops, you would find a shoeshine stand. My brother-in-law, Red Bundy, started out as a teen, shining shoes in Tankins' Barber Shop, and did so for twenty years. When Drug Fair drug store came to town, he applied and began employment as a stock room clerk with all the benefits. My cousin, Big Mo Mosby, trained with the Tankins and later moved to E. Market Street, then on to Bridgewater, Virginia.

Tankins' Barber Shop on Wolfe St. in the 1930s. Image courtesy of Betty Lou Winkey via the Celebrating Simms Project by James Madison University.

After good training, Elon Rhodes opened a shop on East Market Street. Earl Harris also, after training, moved to Luray, VA, and started cutting the hair of colored customers in his shop. Charlie Nickens and Charlie Venny went together and opened their shop when death came to the Tankins.

Harry Lee Solomon also had a shoeshine parlor. It had five chairs with two places for your feet to rest so your shoes could be shined while wearing them. Men kept their shoes and boots shined. It cost like 10 cents to 25 cents, plus tip was expected. Harry Lee had a fruitful business and raised his family of two children along with his wife very well. He bought and paid for his home and worked a second job in a band he created. He was the leader of his band, the Red Dots. Harry Lee played the piano; he had a trumpet player, drummer, saxophone, bass fiddle, guitar, and vocalist.

Bud Byrd had a shoeshine stand in the Harrisonburg parlor. Byrd later moved to Harry Lee's on Main Street and had a five-seat stand. The stands all stayed busy, especially on weekends, Thursday, Friday, and Saturday. The owner, Harry Lee Solomon, worked right along with them. Shoeshine stands were inside and outside of businesses. Whites also kept their shoes shined. Up and down the main street men carried wooden boxes strapped to their backs, and men stopped and got their shoes shined for ten cents.

Mr. Kent Francis had a barbershop on Broad Street in Harrisonburg, in his basement for whites only. Kent also was my son Bill's Godfather. His family lived above the shop; his wife Frances had a beauty shop on the first floor, and her shop was for colored only. Together they did well.

Marion Harris operated a Beauty Parlor on Johnson Street for colored ladies. She was a very popular and stylish lady who did well with her profession.

Harrison Myers owned and operated a barbershop on Wolfe Street. He cut for coloreds, including members of my family. There were two barbers who did not have a shop. They would cut in your home, on your porch, or anywhere. They carried the tools in a barber satchel. Their names were Creed Francis and Stymie Bruce.

Two other barbers had shops in our town, Rawley Bundy and George Blakey. Their shops were from the 1950s through the 1970s. Each had two chairs in their shop, and they were kept busy. George Blakey was our last fulltime barbershop owner and operator and kept alert with the community. He was active in all functions and raised his family well.

No colored barber could cut white women's hair. Colored barbers cut white men's hair in white shops owned by whites but rented to colored barbers. I never saw a sign throughout the community that stated the rules. The rules were simply known. The word "Colored" was used throughout the '30s and '40s and up to the '60s. It was not until rioting in the 1960s that it changed to Black. Black was called beautiful then. I remember James Brown's song called, "Say It Loud I'm Black and I'm Proud." He was truly a role model for social justice in our black community and a businessman, which demonstrated what success looked like.

Elijah Johnson had a shoe repair shop. He was self-trained and had a one-room shop next to his own home. Mr. Johnson did everybody's shoes and was always busy.

Glen's Fair Price was a variety store and in the 1950s was the first white business to hire a colored clerk. The family operated store was very busy and very popular, the only one of its kind in our area. With Jim Crow at a high peak, it was hard to believe how smooth the hiring went. Their hiring of a black clerk did not encourage other businesses to hire blacks. It was much later before that happened.

Jake Johnson had a covered wagon drawn by two horses with canvas in the back where he put ice from the icehouse. Maybe he'd make three trips a day to the icehouse because everyone had iceboxes, and Mr. Jake delivered all over town. Some people went themselves to get ice, but if you did not have transportation or didn't want to walk, you got Jake's ice from his covered wagon.

Northeast Neighborhood resident Charles Newton Strother preparing to enter High Street from West Elizabeth Street. Courtesy of Robert J. Sullivan, Jr. from Nancy Bondurant Jones's Zenda: 1869–1930. An African American Community of Hope.

Mr. Charles Strother, Junior Strother's father, (second from left with a wooden peg leg) was a horse trainer and independent business man who managed Harry Craig Stables in Harrisonburg in the 1930s. Black business men provided valuable services to the community when given the opportunity, even with Jim Crow laws firmly in place.

Erasmus "Razz" Stevenson was one of our own taxi cab drivers. He charged twenty-five cents anywhere in the city. There was also a white cab driver named Robinson, and he charged fifty cents anywhere in the city.

There was a creek and railroad track behind the Imperial Laundry which was fenced in. A sign said in big letters "Help Wanted, White Only." My uncle Frank worked across the street at the Troy Laundry for forty years but they never had a sign. Uncle Frank passed away and they employed two black employees to replace him; but they did not ever put up a White-Only sign at Troy laundry.

Downtown from Wolfe Street, going south and on the left side in the 1940s was a big grey house on the corner. Next to it was a restaurant on Main, owned by a Greek man named George Rontopolous. My uncle was a chef there for many years, and then later went to the Kavanaugh Hotel across the street. The Kavanaugh Hotel was famous for its elegance and beauty; it was very stylish and lavish, was a beauty in the Shenandoah Valley of Virginia, and for whites only.

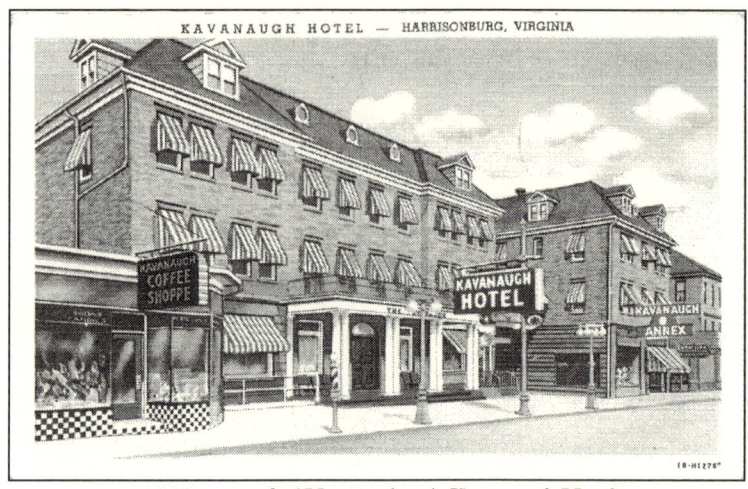

1942 postcard of Harrisonburg's Kavanaugh Hotel

At the Kavanaugh Hotel people of color were hired to cook, be waiters, porters, or shoe shiners. My Uncle Henry Stuart (my mother's half-sister Minnie's husband) was a chef and worked at the Kavanaugh. He never went into any of the hundred hotel rooms, only the kitchen. He came in the back door and went out the back door. He would always give me a piece of pie, whenever I visited, but I had to eat it before anyone came in. I couldn't pay to eat there. It was the law. Even though my uncle was chief cook, I had to go to the back door to see him. I could not buy food there—whites only. The very rich had reservations at the hotel, never people of color and not even foreigners. Segregation was very high in the 1930s and 1940s during my time.

Minnie (Doris's mother's half-sister) with her husband Henry Stuart, their children, and Doris who is on the far right. (c. 1936)

More Downtown and Back Doors

1939 postcard of Friddle's Restaurant on Main St. in Harrisonburg where Doris's aunt and uncle worked.

Beside Friddle's Restaurant where my aunt and uncle worked was the Catholic Church which had one black member, the custodian who cleaned the church and took care of the Father.

Beside the church was the U.S. Post Office. We are now at the corner of Elizabeth and Main Streets still going south; we have a row of department stores (five and dime stores they were called): Charles Store, W. T. Grant, Woolworths, Alfred Ney, B. Ney (two stores), McCrory's Five and Dime, then Meritt's Shoe Store. At the corner of East Market and Main Streets there was the National Bank, Quality Shop Ladies Apparel, Music Store, and Frank's Jewelry Store. These were all white-owned and operated.

The Virginia Theater, our largest of the three in town, had live stage appearances on Saturdays. My sister was a tap dancer as well as my two cousins. Another cousin played drums. They did talent show performances at the theater during intermission.

Next to the theater was People's Drug Store, an alley, Water Street, a shoe store, a drug store, the State Theater, a jewelry store, a gas company, a church, Bruce Street Virginia Craft House, a popular furniture store (all handmade and exclusive), two residents' dwellings to the corner of Franklin Street and Main Street. To the other side going north up Main, there was a famous tea room; there were many such little tea rooms over the city. Next was the Asbury Methodist Church and across Bruce Street there was Buick car dealership No. 3, the Strand Theater, Schewels Appliance and Furniture Store, a famous restaurant, Mick-or-Mack Grocery Store, Hostetter Drug Store, Taliaferro Jewelers, Harry Lee's Shoe Shine parlor (owned and operated by blacks), the First National Bank, and Court Square Street which circles around the Square and the Courthouse.

The Rockingham County Courthouse sits in the center of town. During the 1930s, there was a water fountain in the front yard for drinking purposes with a sign that read "whites only." No blacks even tried to drink from it. What year they removed that sign I don't recall.

On Main Street was a white barber shop that was run by three black barbers. It had a shoe shine stand as well, and that stayed busy. On up the same side still going north was Fletcher's Drug Store, a famous restaurant, and a barber shop. Next was Hawkins Hardware Store and across Elizabeth Street, there was B. Neys Men's Store, Kavanaugh Hotel, next the Wampler Grocery Store, Hayden Dry Cleaners, the Greyhound bus terminal, the Episcopal Church, then right back to Wolfe Street. Incidentally, there were no supermarkets throughout the whole city. There was either a large grocery store or a small one.

We bought groceries at one of our three or four stores mentioned earlier that were within walking distance in the neighborhood. We had to go to town to our only two drug stores to get our prescriptions. One was People's and the other, Fletcher's Drug Store. There was no entrance to the front for blacks so we went up the alley and in the back to People's and on the side for Fletchers. There were signs that read "whites only" in the drug stores on the front and back.

There were "white only" signs on the toilets. There would be a toilet separate in a far-off dark corner or down in a basement for blacks. We also patronized department stores such as Grants,

Charles, Woolworth's, and McCrory's only to purchase what was needed, never to browse. You were watched or followed all the time by the floor manager, which every store provided. You could not try on clothing or shoes, you could never return an article, or get a refund. We had to make sure shoes fit as there was no returning them. Our only shoe stores were Merit's and F. Barth Garber which were more expensive than other stores.

We had department stores and "Five and Dime" stores in our downtown shopping area on Main Street. We had Charles Store, W. T. Grant, Woolworth, and McCrory's, then the better stores like Joseph Ney's, B. Ney, Quality Shop, Charles Fauls, Jimmie's Dress, and a few others.

They each had the same pattern for blacks. As soon as you entered the store, here comes the manager asking, "May I help you?" You did not look and browse. You looked, paid, and got out. Most department stores had a shoe section because they carried the dollar shoes. Someone helped you in putting the shoe on to make sure it fit, as there would not be an exchange or refund. Also, you had to be careful not to handle anything you did not want because if you handled it, you would have to buy. This was the law of all the stores.

We were so used to going to the back door or side doors of restaurants, theaters, drug stores, hospitals etc. We only went in the front door of our grocery stores (owned by colored or white) in our neighborhood. Grocery stores carried very much the same foods until supermarkets came into town.

When you went to the hospital, you walked around the back under dim night-lights whether dark, good weather or bad. We used the back or side door to get to the basement waiting area, which was a hall with benches you sat on waiting your turn for services.

The sign read, "Waiting Room for Colored Only–By Order of Police." In the basement there were eight rooms, two beds to each room and a long closed-in porch with windows all around. The one operating room was on the second floor. There was one restroom for white employees, and another marked "Colored."

Chapter 10
LIFE DURING JIM CROW

Travel and Healthcare

The Greyhound and Trailways buses were our two passenger services through the city for commuting from city to city. They each stopped daily. The Greyhound bus terminal had a big sign over their water fountains. The fountains would be side by side or in the same corner with the words, "← Colored & White →." Anywhere in the state was the same notice wherever the bus stopped. Segregation was imposed.

When boarding, the colored waited until all whites boarded. Then they proceeded to the rear of the bus where there was a bench with a "colored" sign that held five or six people. If the colored section was full, you stood until your destination or until a seat emptied on the bench. Should there be an open seat in the front, never could colored passengers be seated.

Often, my uncle and aunt would travel from Washington, D.C. to Virginia and would have to stand all the way because it was a holiday. Even though a seat might be empty up front, you could not be seated—the Jim Crow law was that no blacks and whites could sit together.

All the drivers were white. Not until the late-1960s and early-1970s did a change in drivers occur. Though President Lyndon B. Johnson signed the Civil Rights Act in 1964 and the Voting Rights Act in 1965 saying all persons could freely go to the theater, ride on public transportation, and attend public schools, the beginning of integration still took several years to come.

Long before the 1930s and after, blacks used the rear entrance of the hospital in Harrisonburg. They could not use the front entrance. My sister, my sister-in-law, and a cousin gave birth in the 1940s. In the fifties, I gave birth to a newborn. We all had to go in the rear door or the side door to enter the hospital to have our babies. The Grace Street side of the hospital had opened adjacent to the Normal School which became Madison College and is now James Madison University. The front side facing Mason Street was still not available to everyone until the 1960s.

Postcard of Rockingham Memorial Hospital from the 1930s. It was originally built in 1911

    Later, five homes (on what was then Cantrell Avenue that runs parallel to Grace Street) were purchased for additional expansion of the hospital. One of the five houses was the home of a family named Burkes. When I was a teenager, I worked for them five days a week after school and a half-day on Saturday.

    After the completion of the addition, an entrance was applied to the Cantrell Avenue side. Since then the hospital has moved and this building has become James Madison University's Health Center. The entrance is still in the same place, but the street is now named Martin Luther King Jr. Way by vote of the people. The new street was named on Martin Luther King Jr.'s 86th birthday in January 2013. It is a fitting name as the front doors that were closed to blacks at the two institutions are now opened to all.

Voting and the Justice System

In Virginia, after 1902, most blacks were denied the right to vote by grandfather clause (laws that restricted the right to vote to people whose ancestors had voted before the Civil War), poll taxes (fees charged to make voting difficult for poor people), white primaries (only Democrats ran for office, and only whites could vote in the Democratic primary), and literacy tests. If you did not read well, you were denied the right to vote. If you owned property, you could get to vote. My parents were property owners.

My parents made a big effort to vote. They planned to be at the polls at 6:00 a.m. every year as soon as the polls opened. They were present and anxious to vote. Being homeowners qualified them to vote. They would talk about voting days before time to go, and we six kids would be excited as they returned home from the polling place to hear all about voting.

Together the two of them marched to the polls and we could not wait until they returned. When I was a grown young lady and married, I thought husband and wife had to go vote together. My husband, Robert Lee Harper, said "No, they do not." He had never heard of it. But then he later agreed that we do go together as family.

My daddy laughed about white men coming around our neighborhood to buy votes for one dollar. They would succeed with some, but not my daddy. He would just laugh at them and say, "No, no." I asked him why he said no. He said, "Always remember this is one privilege that is yours as a citizen of the United States. No one can take it from you. Always remember." And I have.

On our street, my grandmother and my parents owned their homes, which made them qualified to vote. It was not until August 1965 that President Johnson signed the Voting Rights Act into effect, meaning all people, no matter what race, color, or gender, were qualified to vote.

Some states had limitations according to their policies, even though the federal law was that you could vote. If you could not read or write, you could not vote. Many people of color could not read or write. A few did not go to school at all, and some only went to fifth grade. Graduation was in seventh grade in the early 1900s, but there were no ceremonies or exercises.

In the courts, people of color always got stiff fines or more time than whites, and often were whipped with the Billy sticks police carried if you mumbled something. As a little girl, I witnessed such Jim Crow injustices.

The jail is a place of detention for convicted criminals. The jail is also still a place of Jim Crow. There are far more people of color in jails than there are white people. Talking with several inmates who got through the cracks to get out, Jim Crow was present in the big house. As a concerned citizen, previously having paid taxes before retirement, I am a strong advocate of more schools or educational facilities than jails. Good boys go into jails and come out bad men, or don't come out. Good young men go into jails and come out old, bad men.

According to the NAACP "Criminal Justice Fact Sheet," in 2014, African Americans constituted 2.3 million, or 34%, of the total 6.8 million correctional population. African Americans are incarcerated at more than five times the rate of whites.

Jim Crow is bitter, mean, cruel, and still preys on people of color. There is lots of dirty work being done. People of color have no rights, no consideration, no voice. People go in for light charges and are stuck with felonies that hit hard when you hope to vote someday. Restoring their rights makes them free to vote once more. Here in our USA, a new day is born if people with minor convictions are given the right to vote by lifting the felony strapped on them. I salute the governor of VA for stepping forward and clearing the path for our incarcerated.

In April of 2016, Virginia Governor Terry McAuliffe helped to end this unfair practice by signing an "executive action" to lift the lifetime voting ban for those who had been convicted of a felony. This returned the right to vote to more than 200,000 people, many of them black men who had been unfairly charged with felonies at disproportionately higher levels than whites.

Desegregation and My Children's Schooling

The National Association for the Advancement of Colored People (NAACP) decided to challenge the concept of the "separate but equal" law. Fed up with poor, overcrowded, and underfunded schools, black parents in Virginia and South Carolina twice sued the federal government to get children into the better supported and funded white schools. Both times federal courts upheld segregation. Both times the parents appealed.

The Supreme Court agreed to consider the case along with several other similar cases. In May 1954, the nine Supreme Court Justices announced their unanimous decision in *Brown v. Board of Education* that the practice violates the Constitution's Fourteenth amendment and must stop.

When my son Bill was ten years old, he played in little league football at school. That was in the 1960s before the schools had desegregated. He was the only colored to make the all-star team, so he was eligible to play on the championship team. They traveled to Knoxville, TN, for the Turkey —Bill's first out of town trip without family.

The 1966 Harrisonburg Midget League Football All-Stars. Doris's son Bill is number 73 and the only black member of the team. Photo courtesy of Harrisonburg Parks and Recreation.

My son had never been away from our family, but he was anxious to go. The team doctor assured me he would be fine, so I let him go. They played well and won the two games, so on his return home we were excited to hear the stories.

First thing from him was,

Mama, guess what? They did not know there was colored on the team as they had all white. All Harrisonburg team players including me sat on bleachers after we arrived waiting on community folks who were calling out names of my team mates who would be guests of white families. All my team players left the gym, and I stayed by myself for about an hour. Coach kept telling me not to worry about it as they would take care of it. They worked it out, and later a black man, the director of a community center for blacks, came and I stayed at his wonderful home.

Bill stayed with that family for the three nights they were in Tennessee, and he later remembered that it was his first introduction to southern grits. Harrisonburg lost the game, 6 to 18, but still qualified to play in another game, this time in New Jersey, where they beat two teams to become the champs of that tournament.

Upon Bill's return home from New Jersey I was anxious to hear where he stayed as the coach assured me he would take care of everything. Happy and excited, he came home smiling because they had won, and I then asked, "Where did you stay?" He said this time he stayed with colored team parents as they had other colored on their teams so all went well. All the New Jersey teams were desegregated, too, and he had colored families to stay with.

My son continued talking. "Mom, the people in New Jersey were kinder and talked to you more than the ones in Tennessee. Why?" Searching for an answer, I told him that there are all kinds of people in America and all are different. In some parts, they practice a law called Jim Crow, which means "separation of blacks" and you do not associate with each other in any way, as I had said before.

Now, here in our city, a big effort by our recreation department moved slowly into combining our races because integration was coming soon. After a few more years, our president, Lyndon B. Johnson, declared the law that all public schools be integrated as well as public transportation and all public facilities. It is said the Lord works in mysterious ways, his wonders to perform.

To celebrate the courage my son had shown in leaving home for the first time and experiencing how the deep south treated blacks, I surprised him one evening after I got home from working my third job and before I was going to go to my fourth job at 10:00p.m.–2:00a.m. cooking at the Moose Lodge in Harrisonburg. I told him after he finished his homework to get dressed because I had a social justice advocate for Black People I wanted him to meet. We drove to Woodstock, VA and we were the only blacks in the room at the Rotary Club. My son at thirteen years of age had the honor to meet and greet the Legendary Hall of Famer and greatest running back in NFL history, Jimmy Brown. I had a picture that I took of him and Jimmy, but I misplaced it. My son was never the same after meeting Jimmy Brown. He realized that Jim Crow was not going to keep him from being a leader in his community.

Doris's son Bill Harper (circled in center) was one of the early Black students to attend Harrisonburg High School from Lucy F. Simms School after it closed in 1967. Photo from the Harrisonburg High Yearbook, 1968

Chapter 11
REDEVELOPMENT OF NEWTOWN

Harrisonburg Redevelopment and Housing Authority Urban Renewal Project, know as R-4 and R-16, destroyed 60% of the black-owned homes in Harrisonburg in the early 1960s. The open areas, large buildings, and parking lots in the photo above are where most of those houses had been.

The stars mark the locations of Doris's childhood home at 194 Effinger, and the homes of her grandmother and aunt and uncle at 188 and 186 Effinger. All these properties were destroyed during the R-4 phase of Urban Renewal.

Newtown, as it Was

Before Harrisonburg Redevelopment came along, of the twenty-seven families that lived on Effinger street, my parents and my grandmother were the only persons that owned their homes. Other streets also had homeowners. Most blacks owned the homes from Johnson (99% black) to Simms Avenue, and Johnson over to Wolfe Street. From Johnson, out Broad Street to East Elizabeth Street, Mason Street, Rock Street, Federal Alley, Red Hill (Reservoir) were all black residents. Residents owned to Broad, Rock, Elizabeth, and Wolfe. Above Broad were white owners. Federal Alley from Effinger to Wolfe were all black and Reservoir Street, known as Red Hill, was all black. Mason, from Gay to Elizabeth, had a few whites mixed in.

Sometime in the 1950s the Federal Housing Development, along with the city, were knocking on doors informing the residents their property was going to be taken, roads were coming through, and businesses built. We were told that in an area beside the Newtown cemetery, a housing complex would be built and a street would run through to East Market Street. We were unhappy, along with the other residents involved, as they were offering so little and we did not have a choice but had to accept their offer. Most residents were non-owners.

All these houses on the north side of Effinger Street heading down to Blacks Run were destroyed during Urban Renewal.

Of the twenty-seven houses on our street, about eighteen had running water, but that did not mean they all had bathrooms. There were toilets on the closed porches. A private family owned all the houses on Effinger except for two, which were ours and my grandmother's, and she also owned a lot next to her house. Each house had a hydrant in the back yard. Water was piped from the road, and a bill came once a month to that resident. There were problems in winter with freezing and certain ways of wrapping that made it safe to not freeze. Some knew the technique. Others were willing to share water anytime there was a need. The peace and harmony made us happy. Like I said before, we were poor and didn't know it.

Disruption and Relocation

When the Harrisonburg Redevelopment[11] knocked on my parents' door at 194 Effinger Street, I answered the door. Two men approached with a letter saying they were going to buy our property; they remarked that a road will run straight through this property to Johnson Street and, sure enough, it did later on. I called my parents, who were in the kitchen. They were very upset and cried and did not know what to do.

Fortunately, they worked for a white attorney, E. D. Ott at that time, and he advised them what to do, so they got busy. They heard a black doctor on Broad Street was selling his home and moving to Hampton, Virginia. It was always favorable to buy from blacks or get a good white friend to buy for you and then sell to you. So my parents bought the house on 237 Broad Street. My husband and I then moved into that house.

Three or four years later, they bought another house on 314 East Gay Street. Then we moved into that one while my parents

---

[11] *Daily News Record* articles of 1950-1957 show the progression from President Truman's vision for public housing, to Harrisonburg city council's decision to get rid of "blight" in the city. Originally, the plan was to redevelop 36 acres, and relocate 97 families. According to a Jan. 12, 1978 article, however, 200 families were relocated with the redevelopment of 40 acres.
www.publichistory.jmu.edu./urban/dnr.html.

moved into 237 Broad Street. That was their address in 1960 because 194 Effinger Street was being razed by the Harrisonburg Redevelopment Authority.

They bought a third house on 314 East Kelley Street in 1960 for my family, so we had to move again because 314 Gay Street was being torn down for redevelopment. In other words, my parents had to relocate once, and my husband and I had to move twice because of redevelopment. My family and I resided on Kelley Street for years.

Homes not owned were rented privately from two families in the city, the Kleinsteins and the Grattans. They never remodeled or painted and had no inside water so when the housing developers came around, renters thought this a better deal and they were excited. They knew there would be running water, bathrooms, furnace, and a modern-day facility.

Not everyone made the move to the complexes on the hill across from the Newtown Cemetery. Two families that owned bought homes and some moved in with relatives. Some boys of appropriate age joined the armed services of our country.

Effinger Street was next to Kelley's field, owned by John Kelley who lived on a small portion at the bottom of the field right next to Blacks Run. Kelley sold his property to Harrisonburg Redevelopment and later died. An alley between Broad Street and Effinger School was open through to Johnson Street and was later named Community Street. The Effinger Street School, the first black school built in 1882, was demolished and the first stage of the city's plan was in motion. Merchant's Garage and Rose's department store were built with plenty of parking all around the buildings. Effinger Street from Broad to Mason was closed. A dozen more blacks bought land to the east and above the cemetery, within the Newtown area, making it a more rounded out neighborhood.[12]

---

[12] A news clipping from the *Virginia Municipal Review* (Aug. 1961) states that "The citizens of Harrisonburg are well-pleased with their program." For a more realistic insight on the impact of "Redevelopment" on the Newtown residents, see Lauren McKinney's

I can mark the spot where our house stood on the corner of Broad Street and Effinger Street. It was replaced with a new one built. The other corner of Effinger and Broad had the newly constructed Broad Street Mennonite Church. Before the church was built, an apple orchard, along with two cherry trees and several quince trees grew there. They provided food for anyone's tables as we helped ourselves. The church still stands, and the Mennonite congregation welcomes all who will come.

---

article, "Remembering Project R-4" that initially appeared in *eighty-one magazine* (Staunton, VA, 2000). www.worldcat.org/title/71313097

Chapter 11
INTEGRATION AND MIGRATION

The March on Washington

Martin Luther King Jr. (MLK) was born July 15, 1929, in Atlanta, Georgia, and attended segregated public schools. He graduated from high school at age fifteen, went on to Morehouse College in Atlanta and received his B.A. degree in sociology. From there he went to Crozier Theological Seminary in Pennsylvania and received a Bachelor of Divinity (or BD) in 1951. Later MLK got his doctorate from Boston University.

Dr. King married Coretta Scott, and they had two sons and two daughters. He pastored in Alabama and Georgia and was a strong worker in the Civil Rights movement. He became President of the Southern Leadership Conference, an organization formed to seek justice and fairness for all mankind. Writing and publishing books and lecturing all over the south, Martin Luther King became a well-known advocate of racial equality.

Jim Crow was highly visible in the 1950s. King was well aware, and traveled throughout the south, speaking about the discrimination against blacks. Schools were segregated as well as jobs. Blacks had stipulations on voting. No mixing or singing with people of color; the laws were everywhere of what you could do and could not do.

During the 1950s and 60s, I heard of this young man, King, rising up all over the South. I was inspired by his words of deep concern about people in poverty, about people still feeling the chains of slavery, about people in need in general. His speeches were about the struggles and hardships blacks had endured in the past, and that hit hard right here at home. He was loudly and clearly organizing groups of adults and college students. He wanted them to stand up and be accountable, to make a difference. He wanted blacks to vote. He well knew the Jim Crow laws about blacks voting. He was determined to interrupt those laws. All men are created equal, but "justice" in America was not freedom to men of color.

He made me feel down to earth with what he was saying because I was living what he was preaching. Immediately, we began spreading the news of this great man. We were praying, and speaking to friends and family, to our churches, and all throughout the community. "We needed a people movement," and he said just that. In 1963, he and the members of the Leadership Conference decided to march on Washington, DC, with participation from everyone. It was there that his *I Have A Dream* speech exploded. I attended, and what a magnificent turnout to hear Martin Luther King speak to us about jobs and freedom.

On August 28, 1963 there was a bus advertised to go to the March and would leave Harrisonburg from the Presbyterian Church on Maryland Avenue and High Street. I decided to go and took my twelve-year-old son Robert, who stood about five feet, six inches tall, as my bodyguard. The round-trip ticket was $3.50 for each person, and we were told to bring a baggie lunch. The bus was leaving at 7:00A.M. We arrived early and after the bus was filled, we took our seats in the rear of the bus, the same way we had always ridden the bus before.

After being seated on the bus, which was a nice new Greyhound, my son rejoiced over and over. He was excited, not about Martin Luther King Jr., but just to be riding on the bus. I explained to him where we were going and a little about King, but I don't know how much he remembers. He did not have it in school. The thirty-seven seats on the bus were full.

The ride to Washington was quiet. It was all so interesting to be among just whites. There was no friendly exchange of words or gestures to each other. Yet we understood, for it was not my first encounter with the other race. They were polite and kind, exchanging that courtesy. My son had been taught well by his parents and black teachers at Lucy F. Simms School how to associate with white people.

Arriving at the Lincoln Memorial, the crowd was thick and poised, quietly moving toward the Memorial. Free cheese, peanut butter, and water were abundant. People of all nationalities were walking in a calm and serious manner. That was deeply visible to notice. As people moved along, others joined, for they could see they were headed to the Lincoln Memorial. If you had never been there as Robert and I had not been, you would follow the leader because it was a long walk from the buses, which they gave you a written number to return to. There were no restrooms on the buses, but lots of potty houses on the grounds. We were at the fence in front of the stage, looking right up at Dr. King.

There were far more black people than any other race present, but never any difference. It seemed everyone was of one accord. They came for the same purpose, to hear the Rev. Dr. Martin Luther King Jr. When he spoke, his voice roared like the mighty thunder from the heaven above. He spoke of the days gone by. He spoke of the sufferings of the black people. He spoke of

Martin Luther King Jr. at the 1963 March on Washington. Doris noted, "My son bob and I were by the tree next to the stage. Dr. King was looking right at us." Image courtesy of Wikimedia commons

why we were here today. He gave a solution to the problem, which is for "Jobs and Freedom." He said he had been to the mountaintop and now he is on his way down. He said, and I quote: "My struggles have not been easy and yours will not be either," but we should keep peace, and non- violence will pave the way.[13]

Dr. King's speech ended in prayer with a silence I never felt in my life, like a mighty stream that stood still. In his prayer, he gave "thanks to God from whom all blessings flow." He asked God to lead and guide us safely to our destination and that we can go to our individual homes and "Study War No More."[14]

Fifty years later, after the march and his "I have a dream" speech, our northeast section of town voted to name a street in Dr. King's honor. The hospital had expanded its facilities causing another entrance. It was befitting as the doors that were once closed are all now opened onto Martin Luther King Jr. Way.

Other of My Civil Rights Heroes

Ms. Rosa Parks:
Rosa Parks was born Rosa Louise McCauley in Tuskegee, AL, February 4, 1913. She attended segregated schools in Montgomery, AL, including an Industrial School for girls. In 1932, at the age of 19, she married Raymond Parks, barber and member of the National Association for the Advancement of Colored People. With his support she earned her high school degree and became active in the Civil Rights Movement.

---

[13] King's "I have been to the mountain top" speech came later, on April 3, 1968 the day before his assassination. At the March on Washington he did note that freedom would ring from the mountain tops, however. His statement about struggle in his speech was: "With this faith, we will be able to work together, to pray together, to struggle together, to go to jail together, to stand up for freedom together, knowing that we will be free one day."

[14] Though King did use these words "Study war no more" at other times, they were not part of his speech that day. They were, likely, used by others during the march, however.

When boarding a bus, you paid up front, then got off and reboarded at the rear entrance. There was a broad white line at the 3/4 of the bus all the way across the bus. Blacks sat beyond the lines and could not come across the line. Jim Crow.

Signs up saying white only on seats. If all seats were taken, the driver would put white signs on colored seats. Jim Crow.

Rosa made headlines across America when she refused in 1943 to give up her seat and move to the designated back seats for colored. The driver asked Rosa to move, she refused, he called the police, and Rosa Parks was arrested and charged with violation of chapter 6, Section 11 of the segregation law of the Montgomery City Code. She was fined $10 and $4 for court cost. The president of the Montgomery chapter of the NAACP bailed her out the next day. Parks was regarded as having a responsible, mature, quiet, dignified demeanor. She was one of the finest citizens of Montgomery, white or black.

Parks became an icon in the Civil Rights movement and gave freely of herself for the march for justice.

Dr. Maya Angelou:
Maya Angelou was born in St. Louis, MO, on April 4, 1929, with the name Marguerite Annie Johnson. Maya Angelou and Tony Morrison were renowned poets of today. Maya was also a singer, dancer, actor, writer, and producer of plays, movies, and public television. She was a cast member of Porgy and Bess, a coordinator of the Southern Leadership Conference, active in the Civil Rights Movement and worked side by side along with Martin Luther King and Malcolm X. Maya was strongly against the "Separate but Equal" treatment condoned by the federal government, as blacks often felt forced to use inferior facilities or were not offered facilities at all. Jim Crow.

When she was a little girl in Alabama, Maya said she remembered standing on their front porch with her grandmother, and the Ku Klux Klan marching by anytime they wanted to. Jim Crow. Her education began in St. Louis. Then they moved to Stamps, AR, to their grandmother's home on her mother's side. She lived briefly there, then moved on to Oakland, CA. At 14, she attended California Labor School and completed her high school education. She took modern dance classes whenever she could and did well. She later moved to NYC with her son and husband and began to study African dance. She was always writing, and in 1969 wrote her first autobiography, *I Know Why the Caged Bird Sings*. From then on, there were accomplishments over and over. Among other writings, she read her poem "On the Pulse of Morning" in Washington, DC, at the inauguration of President Bill Clinton in 1993.

I was greatly inspired by her poems, which brought together all people of color, of nations, and of denominations, saying come together down by the river side, where the rocks cried out, and we'll study war no more. And still we rise. Maya Angelou died at home on May 2014 in Winston-Salem, N.C.

Working in West Virginia

In the year of 1968, the schools in Virginia had just become integrated. Two of my children that were in an all-black school were placed in the city school at the opening of the year. My daughter graduated from high school in 1968 and my son followed in 1969. She went on to college and my son to the armed services. The younger son, a sophomore in high school at the time, and I went to West Virginia as there was employment there for me.

West Virginia was integrated in schools and employment, but Virginia was not yet integrated in job opportunities. We had family there and they found employment, no problem, for me. My son entered school immediately. Our lifestyle had changed. Everything was not segregated like it had been in Harrisonburg. We had a house to live in and a decent job. With no college degree, there were choices like the hospital, college, restaurants, and maintenance in a school system. I attempted college but suddenly found out I could not work and study. I took a business course and found a job as director of a community center for the city. That lasted twelve years. Then I took a course in early childhood and became an assistant early childhood teacher. After ten years, I became a secretary/clerk for a treatment plant of the city. Again, jobs were more plentiful in West Virginia than in Virginia.

When African students arrived in America with no housing possibilities, Marshall University in Huntington, WV, called my home one day and asked me to help, so I did. At first in the 1970s, I had three students. They bought their own food, and lodging was a small fee. The colleges had not been integrated; therefore, their only alterative was family living. Since my children had gone away to college at the time, that worked for me. One student from Nigeria graduated and went on to Chicago to further his education in med school. Another, after graduation, went to New York City. He was offered a job there, and he had relatives there. The last of the three went back to Nigeria. Their names were Oochie, Elleki, and Jams.

Then there were two brothers from Kenya who came in 1976. Their names were Moses and Joseph Wengi. They did well in college and were so happy they asked could their mother and sister come to visit. I said yes, and oh what a great celebration we had. I learned to cook some of their dishes and they loved mine, but I loved theirs better. After graduating, the boys went to Ohio, one in the bank, the other a manager of Kentucky Fried Chicken who has eleven chain restaurants under his contract.

I never forgot Newtown in Harrisonburg, and with family and mother still living, I traveled these beautiful, almost heaven mountains of West Virginia once or twice a month. I played an active part in Harrisonburg's John Wesley United Methodist Church and was on the membership roll and supported my church well. I was present for activities, weddings, funerals, and any and every annual event.

Living in West Virginia lasted longer than planned—thirty-three years. After retirement from Huntington, I continued to stay in the city, being an activist and full-time volunteer. In 2001, my time in West Virginia was coming to an end; it was time to go home to the Blue Ridge Mountains of Virginia.

Caring, Sharing and Coming Home

From an early age I began doing any and all things for senior citizens, my elders, old folks. When I was ten my mother sent me through the alley three blocks away with dinner for my father's aging brother who was ill and lived alone. Uncle Ernest was retired but had no one to care for him, so mother sent food and I washed his dishes and made his bed when I went to see him. Every Saturday I assisted him with his bath.

On the way to his house, I passed two little old ladies' homes, and sometimes during the week I would stop and see if they needed anything from the grocery store. This was with my mother's approval. Miss Rachel and Miss Turner lived alone and we, along with other neighborhood friends, kept an eye out for them (an Indian saying). My mother was always sending food or clothing to people along with feeding eight of us, counting her and my daddy. Later in life I began to do likewise without realizing I was caring and sharing. I'd look for people who had less than I. My mother's expression was: "Give to those who are less fortunate than you and the Lord will bless you twofold."

Marrying at an early age of twenty-three in 1950, I found myself busy like mother, giving gracefully and looking out for others. At church, there were names on the bulletin board of persons in need, and the preacher announced it openly. Though I was poor and did not know it, like I mentioned earlier, I never let that stop me. My mother would say, "Give and forget you gave—just give and you will be rewarded." Through the years, I have felt that phrase because giving makes you feel good. I began to listen to young people (other than my three children I was raising) earnestly in teaching Sunday School. For twenty years, I followed many young people through to high school along with my children. They were all friends together and stuck together. We were a close-knit family—preacher included. Sometimes their problems took me to court, supporting them which, with the correct procedure, we worked out.

One young lady was married to a fine young man. Sometimes he'd stay out with his buddies too long. He'd come home and run her and the children out of the house, and she would come three doors up the street for help. Either I would go talk to him, or let her and the children spend the night. It went on for a while until he was drafted into the service. Things changed; the children grew up in those four years, but he too grew and began coming home to visit as a loving father. Coming home altogether, he was a changed man. Oh, what a beautiful relationship, and a perfect family began a new Christian journey.

Another little fellow around seven years old came to my house every Sunday to go to Sunday School. I had a station wagon at that time, and I picked up a dozen or so children. He wouldn't wait to be picked up. He knew we ate breakfast before leaving, so he got himself dressed while his Mom was still asleep and came around the corner for breakfast. Sometimes his shoes would be on the wrong foot, or not tied, or his pants not buttoned, but he was clean because his Saturday night bath was taken care of. Today this little fellow has grown into a fine Christian young man and whenever he comes home to visit family, he always remembers me.

One young lady I befriended early in life was married to a professor in college and was expecting her third child. She liked poetry and wrote a lot whenever she could. She did not like to cook, and when she did she left dishes after each meal, so the kitchen was always a mess, which made her husband unhappy and hard to get along with. I talked with her, she made promises (but never kept them) saying she would try to do better. I cooked, cleaned, looked after the children, washed dishes —whatever help I could. I babysat trying to keep peace. I too had a family I took great care of, although they were in their teens. Finally, they were divorced and he supported the children still in school and under age. Meanwhile she sold her first book, then another and began a course at the college plus caring for the children. The children grew like weeds, and she was working hard to help them as they were excelling past their classmates, and together she and I were teaching them good habits along with Boy Scouts and Girl Scouts and all the educational activities available. Their dad visiting, still supporting, played an important part in their raising. At present the oldest has graduated, the next one is second year in college, the baby graduated from high school and plans to attend college.

Another young lady was sick with HIV, and no one would go near her. I made it my duty to comfort her and make sure she had food and water and her meds. I joined the Association and made it possible for her to receive the proper care. Today she is holding her own.

During her thirty years of community organizing in Huntington, WV, Doris Harper Allen had the chance to work with many amazing people. Here she is meeting Muhammad Ali in 1992.

Chapter 12
COMING "HOME"

At retirement I decided to return home to the beautiful Shenandoah Valley. As soon as I arrived here, my sons and daughter had me signed up with the Virginia Mennonite Retirement Center. I joined the VMRC Wellness Center. Then the wishin' and prayin' began to come. I would wish and pray to God that I may reside at VMRC. I stared at the universe and wished upon a star.

My God said keep the faith. After joining, I took part in most activities, attended services, lived in the swimming pool, met lots of friends, kept a little talk with Jesus going, telling him all about my troubles, my desires, my thoughts, talked with staff, found myself way down on the waiting list, but kept the faith and piled on the prayers. I remember in Psalms 27:14 "Wait on the Lord, be of good courage and he will strengthen your heart: Wait, I say, on the Lord."

Guess what? My prayers were answered by God, and VMRC became my new home and has brought nothing but joy, happiness, and peace. I now reside at 1501 Virginia Avenue facing the Blue Ridge Mountains of Virginia in the Shenandoah Valley.[15]

The morning worship theme at VMRC one Sunday was "I learned to be content." Paul in his letter in the Book of Philippians 4:11 wrote, "For I have learned in whatsoever state I am, therewith to be content." I find those words to be comforting this present day here at this community of retirement. I have learned in this past decade to be content, I feel the serenity of humbleness around me. All through my lifetime I have repeated this scripture and found in it that had it not been for the Lord, who is on my side, where would I be? Now I know in keeping the faith which looks

---

[15] Doris Harper Allen continued living at this address until her death on March 4, 2021.

up to thee, I've come a mighty long way. I've lived eight decades of struggle, of peace, of happiness. I've been to the mountain top and I'm coming down. My number one great joy has been seeing the first black President of the United States; this will forever dwell in my heart. I've lived those soon to be eight years of his leadership alert and well alive. My number two great joy, *Brown vs Board of Education* in 1954, the outcome of an extraordinary period in education in our public schools; the book about it rests in my library at home. Number three, I traveled to DC with my 12-year-old son to the March on Washington in 1963. I had been a stockroom clerk for fourteen years at a department store when Dr. Martin Luther King Jr. was assassinated. Another joy was to speak about Dr. Martin Luther King Jr. on his 86th birthday (as I too was 86 years old) at the Memorial Hall at James Madison University. My last great joy was standing before city council in my hometown representing the renaming of a street to Martin Luther King Jr Way.

Final Thoughts

African Americans were treated differently when education began to play a major role in their lives. Their reading, writing, and arithmetic improved and a new world opened before them. Jim Crow began to fade from their lives.

They felt free and human. The more they learned, the more they wanted to learn. They saw a future glowing for their children. Education was the key. It gave you a desire to move up. It made you realize that to excel and become a part of society, you must apply yourself. You could become an inventor, teacher, educator, actor, outstanding citizen, leader in the community. Motivation inspires one to make a new lifestyle and be a role model for our children.

Doris at a Virginia Tech special event with iconic Donna Brazile, an American political strategist, campaign manager, political analyst, and author, along with her niece, Mayor Deanna R. Reed of Harrisonburg, Virginia. Doris said of Deanna, "I am so proud of her accomplishments for our community of Harrisonburg and the Valley."

Education puts you in a category of believers and doers, to think positive and stay focused on the good in mankind. Education is the path to technology which is today the number one score card to living in more preferred surroundings or even going to the moon.

African Americans have gained much respect for their participation in worldly achievements. In some ways it is like Jim Crow never existed. You feel equally treated, you make decisions without assistance, you may arrive at an increased salary level all because you are qualified. My brother Alfred Howard worked twenty years for a public utility company as a janitor. One day his boss came up and said, "I think you deserve a promotion." He increased his wages and gave him a higher-ranking job. He became one of the first electrical lineman in Virginia at sixty. Jim Crow was fading away. However, working as a lineman at sixty was disgraceful.

Education is and continues to make a difference in our society. We are not looking back, though we cannot help but think back. The march forward is greater for all people.

Dr. Martin Luther King said, and I quote, "Education has a two-fold function to perform in the life of men and in society: one is utility and the other is culture. Education must enable a man to become more efficient to achieve with increasing facility the legitimate goals of his life."

Doris Harper Allen began working on her memoirs in the early 2010s and continued through the time of her death. In 2018 she said, "I love working on my books and using the computer technology. Also sending emails. WOW! If we had this ability back in the day. But it's enjoyable to have today!"

MAPS

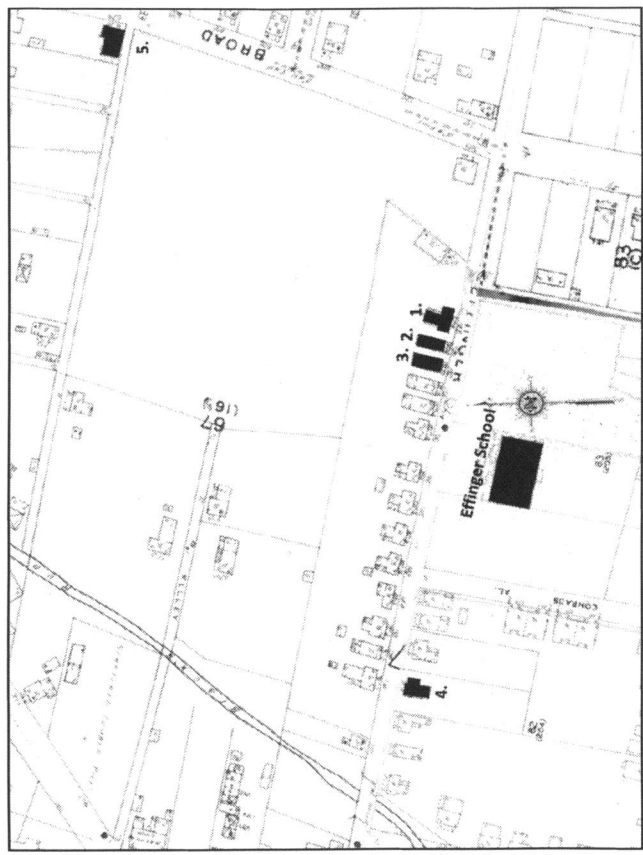

*Map of homes of family member during Doris's childhood.
Modified from the 1930 Sanborn map of Harrisonburg.*

1. 194 Effinger: Leo & Julia Howard, parents to Doris & her five siblings
2. 188 Effinger: Cordelia Howard (Leo's Mother) and Cuetta (Leo's sister) and her three kids
3. 186 Effinger: Frank & Bessie (Leo's sister) Mosby and their seven kids
4. 135 Effinger: Earnest Howard (Leo's half-brother) and his two sons
5. 629 N. Broad: Henry & Minnie (Julia's half-sister) and their two kids

Maps of her Childhood Neighborhood before and after Urban Renewal drawn by Doris Harper Allen

As it was in the 1930s

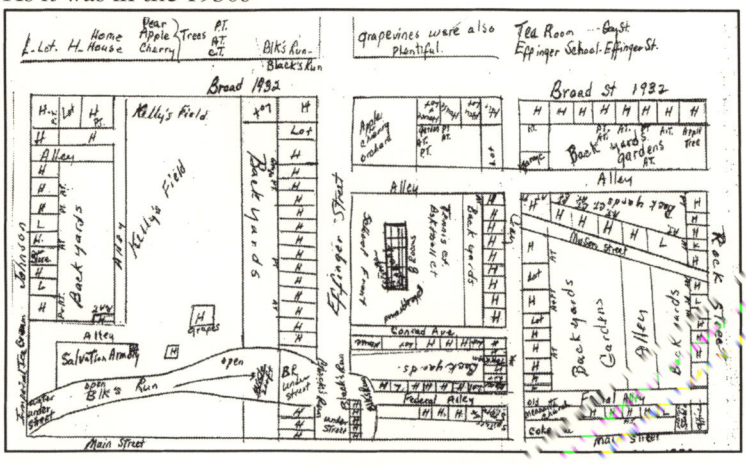

As it was after Urban Renewal

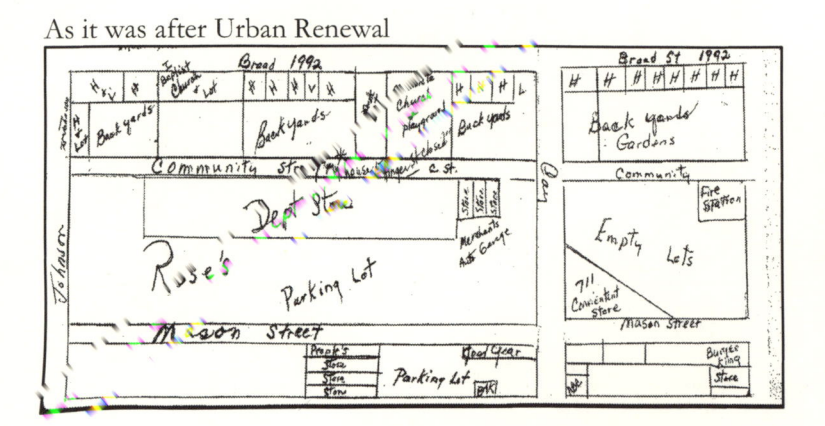

As it was in the 1930s

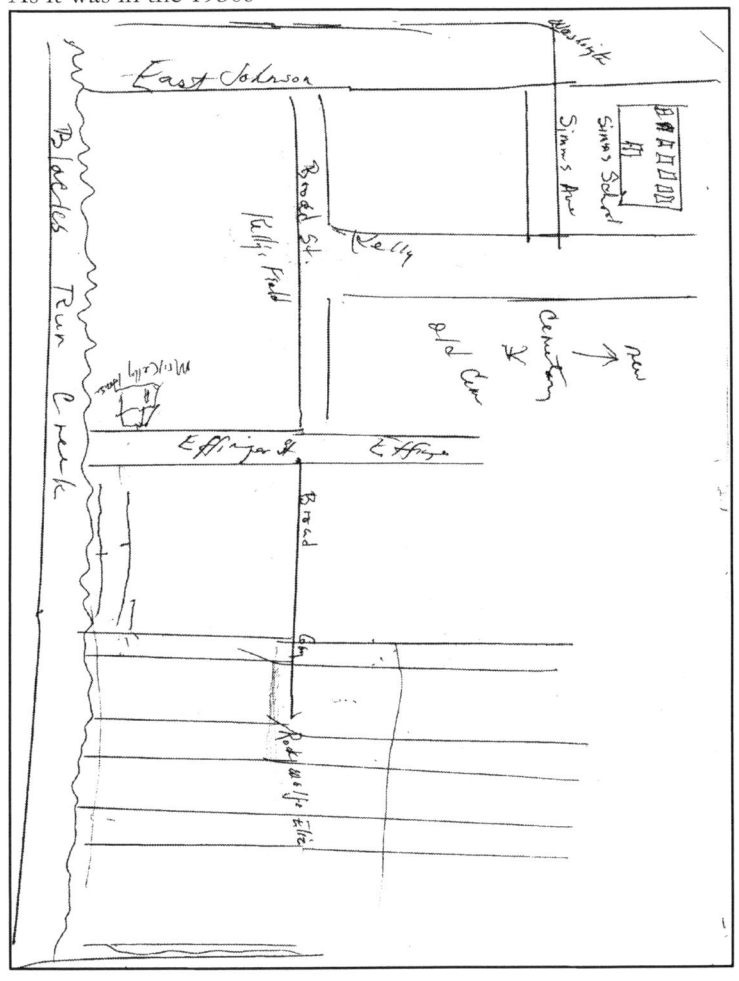

As it was in the 1930s

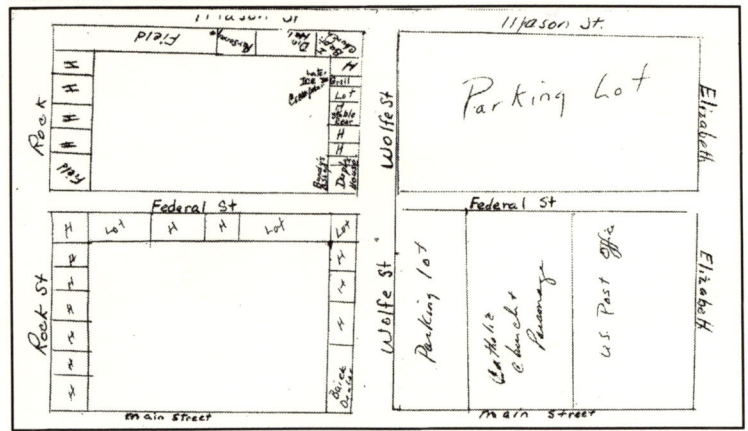

As it was after Urban Renewal

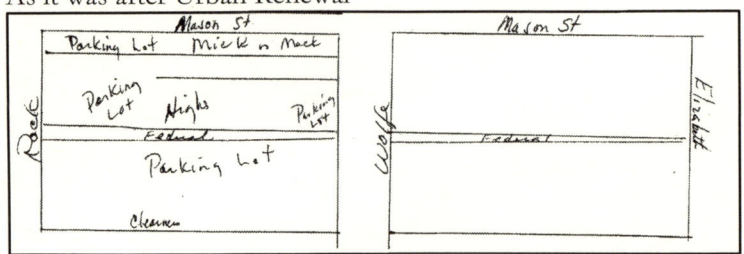

ACKNOWLEDGMENTS
By Doris Harper Allen from her 2015 and 2019 books.

Doris with her sons Robert (Bob) and William (Billo) at the Ibo village reconstruction at the Frontier Culture Museum in Staunton, VA.

Special thanks to my sons Bob and Bill for encouragement and lending an ear to listen. My son Bob is owner and operator of The *Cleaning People, Inc*, a successful (30+ years) small business in the Valley. My son Billo recently started a new tech start-up call *Bilosk*. I taught them early in the 1960s to own and operate your own business, which I learned from my mother and dad, that as black folks always have something you own. Do not think you have to work for anybody but yourself. Jim Crow was real, but in our Newtown community we had black owned businesses in the 1930s, '40s, '50s on to the 1960s. In spite of Jim Crow. I give each one of them a special thanks in their support of my literary journey. Producing two books at 88 and 90.

To my daughter, Belinda, eldest of the three, an Atlanta Schools retired professional. I am ecstatic at the way she orchestrated the individually ordered mailings of my first book, *The Way It Was Not the Way It Is*. That's why Atlanta Public Schools will not allow her to retire. Living in Atlanta, she has her "post office" going full speed in the corner of her garage. When Facebook gave out the addresses, she responded in a cordial manner to immediately send the books quickly on their way without delay.

Doris noted of this picture, "Here is Belinda, me and my wonderful and full of life granddaughter Tiffany, who is an accomplished educator in the Atlanta Public School System. She is unique and special."

To my daughter-in-law P. Thandi Hicks Harper's smiles and encouragement. Her keeping track of details has helped in many ways. We can depend on her for questions and answers. She teaches at Howard University and is committed to students while striving for excellence.

Doris said of this picture "Here is Dr. Hicks Harper and my valley girl granddaughter Thandika, She is a vegan chef. We are a real group when we get together and are always checking folks out."

Imari Searles Harper is my great granddaughter and I thank her for designing my 2019 book's front and back covers. She is very special to me and I am proud of her.

Doris Harper Allen and great granddaughter Imari Searles Harper at the Female Institute for Learning and Development at James Madison University in 2013; Imari received the Best Writer Award. Presently, she is a Graphic Design Artist and owner of her own start-up Illustrated Hustle.

Special thanks to my old school chum "Duffy," who was three grades behind me and we became great friends later in our lifetime. When I told him I was writing a book, he began to gather "oldie but goodies" pictures and newspaper clippings and other past history items, and what great material he contributed. There were names of some I've forgotten, but whom we were both active with during our school days in the 30's, 40's, and 50's. I called Duffy in Luray, VA, (his home) to tell him about my new adventure, and in two days I received loads of materials.

Duffy Smith at age 13 in 1945; the youngest member of BUNDY'S BOYS BAND.

To my school speech-language therapist friend, Dee, who does more for others, especially senior citizens, than she does for herself, and loves it with her bubbling personality of passion. She is gifted with beauty inside and out. Sometimes she wears a ponytail, so I named her Ponytail, and I thank her.

To my Editor-In-Chief for my first book, Esther Stenson, words do not come easy for my devoted editor that has a full-time professional job and finds time to motivate and direct me. She is one of a kind. They do not come great like her.

To my Ace-in-the-Hole, Robin Lyttle, who is knowledgeable and full of kindness and energy that shines above and beyond.

I thank editors Mollie Amelia Godfrey, Shari Weaver and Thandi Hicks Harper for their final review, edits and making a donation of their skilled editorial service. I appreciate unique writers who are special folks that help when needed.

And finally to my Virginia Mennonite Retirement Community (VMRC) who I am thankful to forever, for providing me a culture and community for me to be me and allowing me to share service and love to all.

Doris Harper Allen featured in the VMRC quarterly magazine in 2016.

I give my love to all my friends in Park View and the VMRC community. I have always help those in need.

Doris had a special relationship with the Mennonite Community of Harrisonburg, starting in 1939 when she first attended the Mennonite Gay Street Mission and ending with her residence at the Virginia Mennonite Retirement Community where she spent her final years. She noted, "You must be of service to those who have less than you."

Doris noted: "This is one of my special readers, Paul Rossham. He was one of the first VMRC residents to read my first book, The Way It Was, Not The Way It Is.*" Here he is reviewing a promotional draft of Jim Crow, a book she was working on in her final years.*

51 Steps for God and one of Doris's special bible messages from Psalms 51 Create a pure heart inside me, O God. And put a strong spirit in me.

> **THE WHITE HOUSE**
> WASHINGTON
>
> Happy Birthday! It is a pleasure to join your family and friends in wishing you well on this special occasion.
>
> Your birthday is a wonderful opportunity to survey the past year and look toward future adventures. We hope you enjoy health and happiness in the year to come.
>
> *Barack Obama Michelle Obama*
>
> WWW.WHITEHOUSE.GOV

Politically informed and involved throughout her life, Doris often wrote to political leaders… and sometimes she got unexpected responses! She said of this card, "Even though this letter from The White House wishing me a Happy Birthday may have been computer generated. It was so special to receive my Birthday well wishes. How many of my living friends have received a letter from President Obama and First Lady Michelle? I helped him get elected through the sale of buttons, do not forget that!"

"Know that in life you can always get thru tough times, and be of service to others in your family and community" - Doris Harper Allen

Doris Harper Allen chatting with Mark Metzler Sawin and his Eastern Mennonite University history students about Newtown, 2005.

    Over the past several years, after Doris Harper Allen's health declined, I was honored to be asked by her son, Billo Harper, to help with this project of getting her words out to the world... something that seemed fitting, and indeed essential, in the climate of racial reckoning that emerged after the deaths of Breonna Taylor and George Floyd, and amidst the tumultuous protests over Confederate monuments here in Virginia.

    I thus want to thank Billo Harper for his constant support, energy, and enthusiasm for this project—he is an undaunted promoter of his mother's life and legacy and this project is primarily the result of his energy and drive. I also want to thank Doris Harper Allen's other son, Robert Harper, whose steady, constant presence around her and within this community is deeply felt. His work with the Shenandoah Valley Black Heritage Project, and its long-time champion, Robin Lyttle, a close friend of his mother, helped ground this project.

    Finally, I'd like to acknowledge the numerous members of the Newtown community who have shown a keen interest in this project—their lives are what Doris Harper Allen loved and celebrated, and this love is contagious in her words.

    - Mark Metzler Sawin (January, 2023)

The Gay St. Mennonite Mission summer class of 1939. Image courtesy of Eastern Mennonite Historical Library.

Newtown, Mennonites, and the 1939 Gay St. Mission Photograph

By Mark Metzler Sawin

In the process of working on Doris Harper Allen's memoirs with her son, Billo Harper, another project also emerged. The remarkable image to the left—one taken in 1939 at the Gay Street Mennonite Mission in Harrisonburg, Virginia, includes Doris Jean Howard, the then 12-year-old girl who would grow up to become Dr. Doris Harper Allen. When she began working on her memoirs in the 2010s, Mrs. Harper Allen came across this image and loved it. Then, as part of the process of compiling her memoirs over the past few years, her son Billo and her great-granddaughter, Imari Searles Harper, artistically recreated this image adding color and text (see the colorized version on the back cover of the book).

This image is profound because it tells a deep story of two communities who for decades lived side-by-side but nearly completely separate in the Shenandoah Valley. But as this photo illustrates, in the 1930s, these two "outsider" groups began to mix. Their interactions challenged the mainstream culture's ideas about race, while also challenging the core assumptions of both the black and Mennonite communities themselves. Doris Harper Allen was a part of this early Mennonite mission in Newtown, and she spent her final days at the Virginia Mennonite Retirement Center. She also spent her life crossing and breaking the boundaries that are also very much a part of this image. It thus seemed fitting to add this brief essay about these two communities here at the end of her memoir. But to understand this powerful picture, it is necessary to first step back and place it within its complex cultural context—something Doris Harper Allen navigated throughout her life.

Mennonites first came to the United States in the 1680s, and after initially settling in Pennsylvania, they migrated down through Maryland and into the Shenandoah Valley of Virginia by the 1730s. Mennonites viewed themselves as "in this world, not of this world," but this was a belief that only extended to some aspects of life. They kept to themselves socially, rarely mixing in friendship or marriage beyond their church communities, and they strictly avoided state and national politics and any form of militarism. However, when it came to commerce and trade, they largely engaged with the wider world, growing and processing crops for trade and actively engaging in business pursuits from milling and woodworking to the industrial production of pottery, furniture and other durable goods. This was true in all areas of the United States where Mennonites settled, but in the Shenandoah Valley things were a bit different because, unlike their brothers and sisters who stayed in Pennsylvania or who migrated to other northern states like Ohio and Indiana, Mennonites who settled in Virginia found themselves in the midst of a slave-holding culture.

Virginia Mennonites did not condone slavery among their members because enslavement required coercion and force which stood in stark contrast to their understanding of Jesus's teachings—indeed shortly after they arrived in the New World, Mennonites joined with their fellow pacifist Quakers in signing one of the earliest anti-slavery documents in 1684. But this did not mean that Mennonites were abolitionists or supporters of African American rights. Most Virginia Mennonites passively condoned slavery and, indeed, benefitted from the enslaved labor used by their neighbors—labor that they likely used as well through the rental of enslaved labor. So though they saw themselves as separate from American society, as Swiss-German immigrants, Mennonites in the Shenandoah Valley automatically gained a huge advantage—they were defined as white. This meant that they, unlike their non-white neighbors, could buy and sell property, open businesses, freely move, and after 1789 enjoy all the "blessing of liberty" promised and protected by the Constitution of the United States. So though Mennonites largely shunned all involvement with the state, they benefit heavily from it. They did refuse to participate in the direct, violent subjugation of people, whether through wars against Natives or the enslavement of Africans, but as white citizens, the violence of the state benefitted them all the same, allowing them to gain land, acquire wealth, and achieve high levels of security—things that they, like their slave-holding neighbors, eagerly, actively, and readily embraced.

At the time this photo was taken in 1939, African Americans had been living in Rockingham County for two centuries, having come to the region when slave-holding families began pushing west beyond the Blue Ridge mountains and settling along the fertile banks of the North and South forks of the Shenandoah River. Early census records show that in the 1810s and 1820s African Americans made up about 14% of the population—seven out of eight of them were enslaved, but one in eight (12.5%) were free. As the county's population grew over the next two decades, African Americans remained at about 14%, but a greater percentage gained freedom—almost one out of every five black residents (19%) were free by the 1830-1840s.

During these same years, Virginia's population as a whole was almost half black (49%), and 91% of them were enslaved. This meant that Rockingham County was far whiter than the majority of Virginia, and that its black population was more than twice as likely be free. Thus, when Union troops finally captured the Shenandoah Valley in 1864, and once the 13th, 14th, and 15th amendments ended slavery and brought about citizenship and voting rights over the next five years, African Americans in the Harrisonburg area were faced with the same prejudices and obstacles all freed slaves faced, but they were also in a position to make more rapid progress than in many other parts of the South.

By 1870 black families had acquired property in the northeastern section of Harrisonburg and founded a school and several churches in what became known as "Newtown." In the 1870-1880s this community and the majority white population of Harrisonburg knew each other well. Most of the black population had grown up enslaved by white households, and though it was rarely acknowledged, it was commonly known that many of them were half-siblings of the white children of those same households—1850 census data listed one in five (19.8%) of the enslaved population in Rockingham county as "mulatto" meaning of mixed black and white ancestry. But as the decades went by, the brutalities and realities of the slave era that created this cruel but real intimacy between Harrisonburg's black and white citizens faded. By 1890 segregation had become the norm as unwritten rules of conduct restricted the business and daily interactions between these two communities, completely separating their social circles. By 1896 the *Plessy vs Ferguson* Supreme Court ruling made "separate but equal" the law of the land, and in Rockingham County this played out by strictly limiting where African Americans could live, where they could shop, and what jobs they could have. "White Only" signs went up at train stations, at business entrances, in hotel lobbies, and over the water fountain in the courthouse square.

The strict segregation of blacks from white society that became law in the 1890s expanded throughout the following decades, and African Americans began losing many of the rights they had gained in the decade after the Civil War as they were increasingly stripped of their rights and bared from civic participation.

During that same time, Mennonites were also undergoing a separation from society, but in a very different form—their separation was self-imposed. As "modern" ideas began to emerge and new modes of dress, transportation, and consumption of goods began to increase in the United States, Mennonites chose to emphasize their unique religious identity by adopting strict rules on dress and conduct. They adopted distinctive head coverings and cape-dresses for women and collarless plain suits for men which made them easily recognizable to the community at large. Further, their low-German speech and refusal to participate in the patriotic surge that came with World War I caused many mainstream Americans to see them as subversive and un-American. They thus became an "other" group within mainstream white America.

Mennonites embraced this self-imposed exile, building communities and institutions of their own away from their other white neighbors. In Harrisonburg, they settled to the north of town in a small community they called Park View but that most residents, black and white, simply referred to as "Mennonite Town." In 1917 Mennonites established their own academy to educate their youth—Eastern Mennonite School. So it was that between the 1890s and the 1930s, two distinctive groups, the African Americans in Newtown, and the Mennonites in Park View, lived lives close to but largely separated from the mainstream white population of Harrisonburg, and from each other.

Though both these "other" communities were geographically close to one another, they did not relate largely because Mennonites defined themselves as "white." In Virginia this meant that they upheld segregation—the rules of their churches and institutions enforced racial segregation even while rejecting many other laws and customs such as participation in the military and voting. But the morality of segregation soon came into question. In 1924 two "*mulatto girls*" from the Thompson family applied for membership in a local Mennonite church. Ultimately the Virginia Mennonite Conference decided they could become members, but not before they offered "*a word of caution against integration and fellowship which should not be too intimate*." But even with this ruling, the Thompson sisters were delayed for a year, but when they persisted the conference gave its final approval and they were baptized Mennonite in 1925, making them the first non-white Mennonites in Virginia. But with this decision, the Virginia Mennonite Conference also noted that they opposed "close social relationships" and "marrying between the colored and white races."[1]

About five years later, an Eastern Mennonite School student named Thelma McConnell began visiting Newtown each Sunday, and by 1935 she and her fellow members of the Young People's

---

[1] Thompson girls story from Harry A Brunk, *History of Mennonites in Virginia 1900–1960* vol 2 (Verona, VA: McClure Printing, 1972), 353. Marriage restrictions from Tobin Miller Shearer, *Daily Demonstrators: The Civil Rights Movement in Mennonite Homes and Sanctuaries* (Baltimore: Johns Hopkins University Press, 2010), 134.

Christian Association (YPCA) began conducting what they called "Cottage-Prayer Meetings" on a regular basis. They asked the conference for help with these efforts and in May of 1936 they were granted funds to rent a space in the neighborhood where they began holding services for both blacks and whites, though at different times. In 1936 they began a summer bible school there and Rowena Lark, an African American Mennonite convert, helped to run it. Rowena had joined the Mennonite church in Pennsylvania in 1927 and later her husband, James, became the first African American Mennonite pastor.[2]

This new mission quickly proved challenging to local Mennonites because its membership included both blacks and whites— something taboo to the segregated culture of the South which most Virginia Mennonites also firmly supported. So, just five months after the Virginia Mennonite Conference rented its initial building (the one pictured on Gay Street), it acquired a second one on Chicago Ave in October of 1936, moving its white mission to that space and maintaining the original location as its black mission. But things again became complicated in 1938 when the Gay Street Mission began making inroads into the adult African-American community.

Up to that point services had been primarily limited to children's bible school and Sunday school sessions with little interest or involvement from adult residents. But when YPCA members began to reach out toward adults, and when those adults began to respond, white Mennonite leaders became uncomfortable "because of problems connected to church membership for them." Some proposed closing the mission, but they ultimately decided to wait a year and see what happened.

Upset with this decision and determined to push toward a more integrated church, Ernest Swartzentruber, the 27-year-old superintendent of the colored mission, invited a teacher from the Eastern Mennonite School, Ernest G. Gehman, to begin a series of evangelistic meeting there on Christmas day, 1938. Rowena Lark also continued to be a strong and controversial presence; she dressed in more conservative coverings and cape dresses than

---

[2] Shearer, *Daily Demonstrators*, 33-35. James Lark was ordained in 1946.

most white Mennonites in the area, thus firmly asserting her connection to that community, but while wearing this modest garb, she also delved into her African American religious traditions, singing solo spirituals at the mission church. Even more controversially, instead of just reading children's stories to the youth, she gave "stirring messages" to the community at large—in other words, she *preached*. This was an activity forbidden to women in both the Mennonite and in most black churches at that time. Further, Lark's friendship with Ernest Swartzetruber's wife, Fannie, also became intimate and close—they treated each other as family—and this closeness was uncomfortable for many in both communities.[3]

These were the social, racial, religious, and cultural dynamics that colored the moment this picture was taken in the summer of 1939. The artistically newly colored version of this image highlights these historical realities, but also reveals the hopes, desires, and aspirations that continue to drive these two communities today. The image shows the segregation of the time—white Mennonite adults with the black children of Newtown. White children are not present, and indeed it would not be until the mid-1960s that black and white children would attend the same public schools in Harrisonburg. And black adults from the Newtown community are also not present, for the segregation strictures of the day prevented black and white adults from easily associating with each other. But at the same time, the image shows the beginnings of a new reality. Along the back row at the right we see Ernest Swartzentruber standing, the idealistic leader of this mission who championed a world where black and white people joined together as brothers and sisters, and next to him stands Rowena Lark, an African American convert to the Mennonite faith and a close friend of the Swartzentrubers who was willing to challenge the norms of both the black and Mennonite community in the cause of a more inclusive world.

In the years after this picture was taken, relations between Harrisonburg's black and Mennonite communities continued to grow amidst America's Jim Crow laws and culture that influenced

---

[3] Shearer, *Daily Demonstrators*, 30–42.

all interactions. Several black families joined the Mennonite church, and their demands to be treated equally and justly pressured white Mennonites to move toward more inclusion. Though there was much opposition, Eastern Mennonite School began accepting black students in 1948, making it one of the first historically white schools in the South to desegregate. Meanwhile many of the young people in this picture went on to push against the restrictions of Jim Crow, becoming prominent professionals, advancing in academic and business spheres, and helping to drive what became the Civil Rights movement of the 1950–1960s. This picture thus shows both a point of potential and hope amidst the cruel restraints of the Jim Crow laws of its era, while also still illustrated those same cruel divisions that kept blacks and whites divided. The new imagining of this image by Doris Harper Allen's son and great-granddaughter shows the power and resilience, the hope and potential that drove her life, and that continues to drive the efforts of these communities to became *a community*—one that truly embraces diversity, equity, and inclusion for all.

A photo taken the same day in 1939 of some of the kids at the Gay St. Mission. Nearly 12-year-old Doris is on the far right in a bonnet. Courtesy of Eastern Mennonite University Historical Library.

Artistic rendering of the 1939 Gay St. Mennonite Mission photo by Billo Harper. See color version on back cover of book.

Appendices

VOICE OF THE COMMUNITY

During her many years of civic work in both Harrisonburg, VA and Huntington, WV, Doris Harper Allen frequently wrote editorials in the local papers in support of causes she felt were important, and to call out wrongs that needed to be corrected. This form of activism was recognized by local editors. Below is a letter of commendation from the Huntington Herald-Dispatch *followed by a series of articles written by Doris Harper Allen.*

herald-dispatch.com
HUNTINGTON, WV

Allen Proves Worth of Public Journalism
March 1996

Doris Allen is the best argument I know for public and community journalism.

This remarkable and generous woman's story of community and family involvement went untold by the local media for almost 30 years. Allen was this year's winner of the Black Leadership Award, and her story was finally told.

For 27 years in Huntington, she has raised her children, and, when necessary, raised a little Cain. That part I know well.

She has been a member of *The Herald-Dispatch's* Reader Advisory Board for much of my time as executive editor. She is direct, to the point, and far more often than not, she's on target. When she speaks, I listen, because I know it will be important.

When you read the listing—albeit incomplete—of her accomplishments and service, it is simply amazing that she has not been the subject of feature stories in the past.

It's sad, but true: We missed her story because we have not been close enough to the community, specifically not close enough to the minority community. I do believe that is changing.

Many of you have noticed that the newspaper is moving away from institution based. We are moving away from letting officials alone determine what is news, and isn't news, and toward having citizens define what is important to cover.

Our approach to news coverage is to get involved at the community level, to get to know what's important by being a part of the community, and by bringing more citizens into our newspaper.

That's why we have been and will continue to be involved in public discussions on important issues, including racism and education, and it's why I encourage staffers to get involved in the community, outside the newsroom. That's a change for newspapers, and its fairly controversial among journalists. The case against public journalism is that journalists, by tradition, are trained to be detached and uninvolved, in theory to protect their objectivity.

Those of us who believe in public journalism need to go no further than Allen to state our case. We missed her story for three decades because we valued our objectivity above our community, because we case ourselves separate and apart from our readers.

I think it is long past time for change, and this newspaper intends to be a leader in that change.

In this case, I think other issues probably where involved, too. People in the media, like people in other jobs, tend to spend their off-hours time with those like themselves. That's an argument for greater diversity in media staffing, and frankly, in other public and private offices as well.

Doris Allen is one of the good people on this Earth, a real community treasure. Now, finally, everyone in our region knows it, too. I'm only sorry that it took so long.

- Robert C. Gabordi is executive editor of *The Herald Dispatch*.

VOICE OF THE PEOPLE

We need to wipe slate clean on City Council

An excellent picture was shown on the front page of The Herald-Dispatch on June 11.

If anyone is "impeached," it should be the clowns of City Council — not just one, but all of them.

We need to wipe the slate clean and get pleasant positive thinkers with pleasing personalities and business minds where their works will show.

This sorry statement about people on "fixed incomes" has got to stop — some of them live like kings and queens.

Some don't want help, some are overhelped.

Ask me, I am in the marketplace and know some by name.

If junk food costs $2 or more and they want it, they get it. Some folks on fixed income are junk foods' best customers.

Council does not have a solution to the problem — "impeach them." Every idea, every answer given, council slam bams.

Now, don't let me hear you say you thought I was your friend. I am, but business is business. Huntington, or any town or city, needs a plan and a coordinator to pull in jobs, create jobs, save jobs and boost business.

We have persons who have that expertise and have shown success. But leave it to council to either table it or vote no. "Impeach them."

Council needs a group of young, aggressive, clear-minded doers. Then Huntington will roll on with its leader.

Doris H. Allen
Huntington

Police 'rookies' need sensitivity training

As a concerned citizen of Fairfield West, I am appalled at the rudeness of our police officers.

My church on 18th Street was the setting of a gorgeous black and white wedding May 13.

The bride and groom (grads of MU) were traveling west on 3rd Avenue in a Mercedes Benz en route to a reception.

The bride's parents parked their car, went into reception, waited a few minutes, looked out, saw flashing lights in the next block and went to inquire.

It was the bridal couple approaching the first officer in the cruiser.

The mother touched the Mercedes. The officer roughly said, "Stay back." He then got out of the car and quickly apologized. The bride's father and the nervous, upset, tearful couple found out the officer had asked for a driver's license and was calling Georgia for verification. (The groom was from Atlanta.) The father spoke to the officer, who hung up the phone and said it was OK to go.

Calvary Baptist Church had an all-day seminar last month with department officials from Charleston on "what to say if stopped by police."

We need a seminar on what you do to not get stopped by police.

For minorities, the system is not changing. There is a need for daily sensitivity sessions for these "rookies" from officer training school. They are young, intimidating, forceful and rude. This was an embarrassment to a reputable family, our Fairfield West citizens, plus our out-of-town guests.

Doris H. Allen
Huntington

Neighborhood facing drug problem again

In regard to Brother Reginald Hill's letter to the editor on July 31, I need to speak out.

I've been a deeply concerned taxpaying citizen for over 30 years.

Two years ago, for two years we fought drug invaders on my block day, night, holidays etc.

The task force and the police department were constantly called and finally the street was cleared and cleaned.

That was two years ago. Now the invaders are back strongly armed with prostitutes of both races.

Many calls to law-abiding services have not resolved the situation, because the officers want name, color, make, model, year of car, license number, person, sex, big, small, wearing apparel etc.

It is impossible to obtain all that in trying to observe, therefore people are hesitant in reporting.

Officers made big busts two weeks ago, but there's no no change.

Where do we turn? City Hall? Council? Where?

We want our peaceful community back our children need to play outside not stay inside.

Doris Allen
Huntington

Mayor Rogers Should Be Praised

AS A native of Harrisonburg, I salute Larry Rogers for his honesty, dedication and integrity, which has earned him the title of "mayor" of the city of Harrisonburg.

Moving home 18 months ago from Huntington, W.Va. after 35 years, this was a deserving move in today's direction. Huntington had its first black mayor 15 years ago, after he served council for eight years and I am pleased to see this honor served in our city.

I am a concerned senior citizen, a registered voter of the community and look forward to giving Mayor Larry Rogers encouragement as well as support.

My two sons, Bob and Bill Harper, join me in this congratulation.

Doris H. Allen
Harrisonburg

Appearance in Cosmo

Old Ladies Who Really, Really Want to See Hillary Clinton Become Our First Female President

DORIS HARPER ALLEN, 89

HARRISONBURG, VIRGINIA

On October 5, 2106, in the run-up to the election, Cosmopolitan *journalists Kathleen Kamphausen and Prachi Gupta wrote a story featuring "old ladies" who were strongly in support of Hillary Clinton as the first female president. One of the ten women they featured was Doris Harper Allen. Here is what she said:*

In 1945, segregation had the doors locked, and I was 180 miles from the only black college around for miles and miles around. My parents couldn't afford it. But I educated myself along the way by attending educational sessions, and I attended a couple universities, and I attended a college in West Virginia. I just attended, I didn't complete. There's been a lot of barriers broken, but there's still segregation in America. [I noticed Hillary Clinton] when she and Bill were first in the White House. I saw then that she was an organizer and a leader. I want her to do what she promised to do, to find jobs. These kids need jobs, we need to get them off the street. And we don't need to fill any more jails; we need to build schools. As a senior, I feel that she has a lot of experience, that I have lived through some of what she has come through. It will mean the world to me to see [her elected president], because it will be a giant step for us women in America. We have come a long way, and it's all because we put a fight for everything we earned, and she will prove to us that we can, that we will.

The full article is available at: www.cosmopolitan.com/politics/a4311932/hillary-clinton-supporters-older-females/

Honorary Doctoral Degree

During its graduation ceremony in 2019, James Madison University granted Doris Harper Allen an Honorary Doctoral Degree in recognition of her years of service to the community, and to acknowledge the injustices done during the era of segregation when she and all other African American students were barred from entering the university.

These are the remarks made by JMU President Jonathan R. Alger at that ceremony.

From time to time, James Madison University extends its highest honor by bestowing honorary doctoral degrees on outstanding individuals. This is the university's way of paying special tribute to individuals whose contributions to society are at the highest level. It is an honor that James Madison University does not take lightly.

Although the University awards more than 5,000 degrees every year and has awarded nearly 128,000 degrees since its founding, we have presented only 34 honorary doctorates in our entire history. Today, we are very proud to add Doris Harper Allen to this select group of men and women.

Doris Harper Allen has a remarkable American story and is the very embodiment of engagement. Sadly Ms. Allen was once barred from attending Madison College due to the racial barriers of the time, but today we are proud to have her as a partner to JMU faculty and students.

Instead of pursuing her studies back then, she wound up working in the catering industry in Harrisonburg — eventually serving as the cook for JMU President G. Tyler Miller.

Doris left to attend Marshall University in the early 1970s, but the needs of the community drew her to set aside her own studies and serve others. For 20 years she served the Huntington, West Virginia community as an assistant early childhood teacher, as the executive director of the Scott Community Center, and as a board member of the A.D. Lewis Boys and Girls Club.

Fortunately for all of us here, Ms. Allen returned to Harrisonburg and continued her commitment as a community leader. She has been deeply involved in revitalization efforts in the Northeast neighborhood and was a critical voice in the renaming of Martin Luther King Jr. Way.

As a historian of our area, Ms. Allen has published two important books (a memoir and a history) that provide unprecedented insights into the racial landscape of 20th-Century Harrisonburg.

She has shared her experiences with countless faculty and students — including working with Drs. Mollie Godfrey and Sean McCarthy on their project "Celebrating Simms" — which resulted in a permanent exhibit celebrating the impact of the Lucy Simms School. She collaborated with Dr. David Ehrenpreis to put together a program on the impact of urban renewal projects on the Northeast Neighborhood in Harrisonburg, and her book is required reading in the class he is teaching about 1950s and 60s Harrisonburg.

She has demonstrated the heart of an educator, both through her written works and in conversations about her experiences that have enriched the lives of students, faculty members, and the entire community.

Along the way Ms. Allen has been recognized with the Huntington Black Professional and Business Women's Award; the Carter G. Woodson Ph.D. Award (for commitment and dedication to HIV/AIDS Prevention); the Shenandoah Valley Hit Newspaper Distinguished Female Community Service Award (for outstanding contributions to the Shenandoah Valley); the Fifth District of Electra Prince Hall award (for dedicated service of over 60 years); the Huntington NAACP's Freedom Fund Lifetime Achievement Award in 2017; and (my personal favorite) the Black Girls Rock award from JMU's Lambda Chi Chapter of AKA in 2017. (That means she is officially really cool!)

Doris Harper Allen should have been a student at Madison College many years ago, and that history of a segregated society and university is something that we must not forget. Today, however, we can welcome Ms. Allen with open arms and bestow upon her our highest honor.

Therefore... By the authority vested in me by the Board of Visitors of James Madison University, I hereby confer upon Doris Harper Allen the degree of Doctor of Humanities

The Harper family gathered around Doris Harper Allen after her Honorary Doctoral Ceremony at James Madison University in 2019.
Back Row: Bob Harper, Jennifer Wilson, Thandika Harper Hicks Wilson, Sylvia Quinton, Belinda Harper, Deanna Reed, Billo Harper
Front Row: P. Thandi Hicks Harper, Doris Harper Allen, Tiffany Harper Hodo

DORIS HARPER ALLEN IN THE NEWS

Northeast Neighborhood resident Doris Harper Allen guided EMU students into local history each summer[4]

Doris Harper Allen, 88, greeted a group of Eastern Mennonite University (EMU) students in the parking lot of Rose's in Harrisonburg, the former heart of Newtown. She quickly passed out laminated maps of what is now known as the Northeast neighborhood, and then flashed a vibrant smile from beneath her bright red sunglasses.

---

[4] https://emu.edu/now/news/2021/northeast-neighborhood-resident-doris-harper-allen-guided-emu-students-into-local-history-each-summer/

James Madison University Renames Building in Honor of Doris Harper Allen and others[5]

Doris Harper Allen (1927-2021)

Allen grew up in Harrisonburg. Unable to attend the segregated Madison College as a student, she settled as the cook here at Hillcrest, the President's house, where she managed events from family dinners to official receptions. During her lifetime, Allen became a prominent local historian, author of two books and community activist for diversity, equity, and inclusion. She and son attended March on Washington in 1963. She was a member of the Order of the Eastern Star fraternal organization and was awarded the NAACP Freedom Fund Lifetime Achievement Award in 2017. JMU awarded Allen an honorary doctorate in 2019.

---

[5] This story was covered by multiple media outlets. See Nick Anderson, "Three JMU buildings once named for Confederates now honor African Americans," *Washington Post* (Feb. 19, 2021). Available at: www.washingtonpost.com/local/education/jmu-buildings-confederate-renaming/2021/02/19/107a2200-72f8-11eb-85fa-e0ccb3660358_story.html

Dr. Doris Harper Allen Day recognized by the Virginia Mennonite Retirement Community

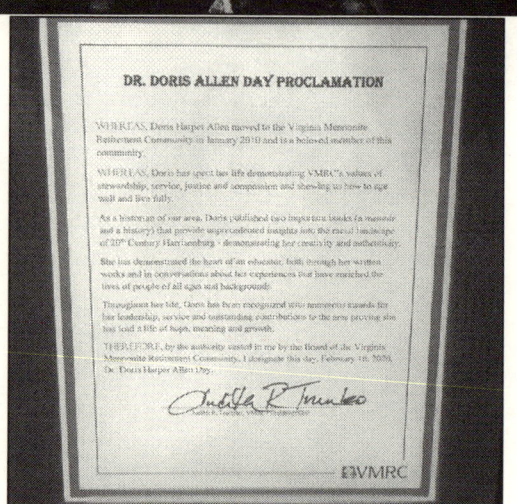

The BodkinRose Law Firm of Harrisonburg, VA presented Doris Harper Allen with a framed picture of Lucy Simms, in acknowledgements of her longtime dedication to the neighborhood that both she and Simms had served. Doris Harper Allen was also the last-living student of Lucy Simms.

Doris Harper Allen with Judge John A. Paul of the 26th General District Court & Meeting Leymah Gbowee, 2011 Nobel Peace Prize laureate & EMU alum

221

Rev. Brown, Al Jenkins founder of Long's Chapel Restoration, and Doris Harper Allen with JMU Students. Long's Chapel, built c. 1870 served as both a church and school for the Zenda Community just north of Harrisonburg, a settlement began by formerly enslaved families shortly after the Civil War. Lucy Simms first taught at this school.

Doris Harper Allen at the Celebrating Simms Exhibit. She served as an advisor to this JMU sponsored project.

Doris Harper Allen discussing her first book as a guest speaker at the African American Female Academy of James Madison University

Doris Harper Allen leading a discussion of her book at Sandy's Book Club

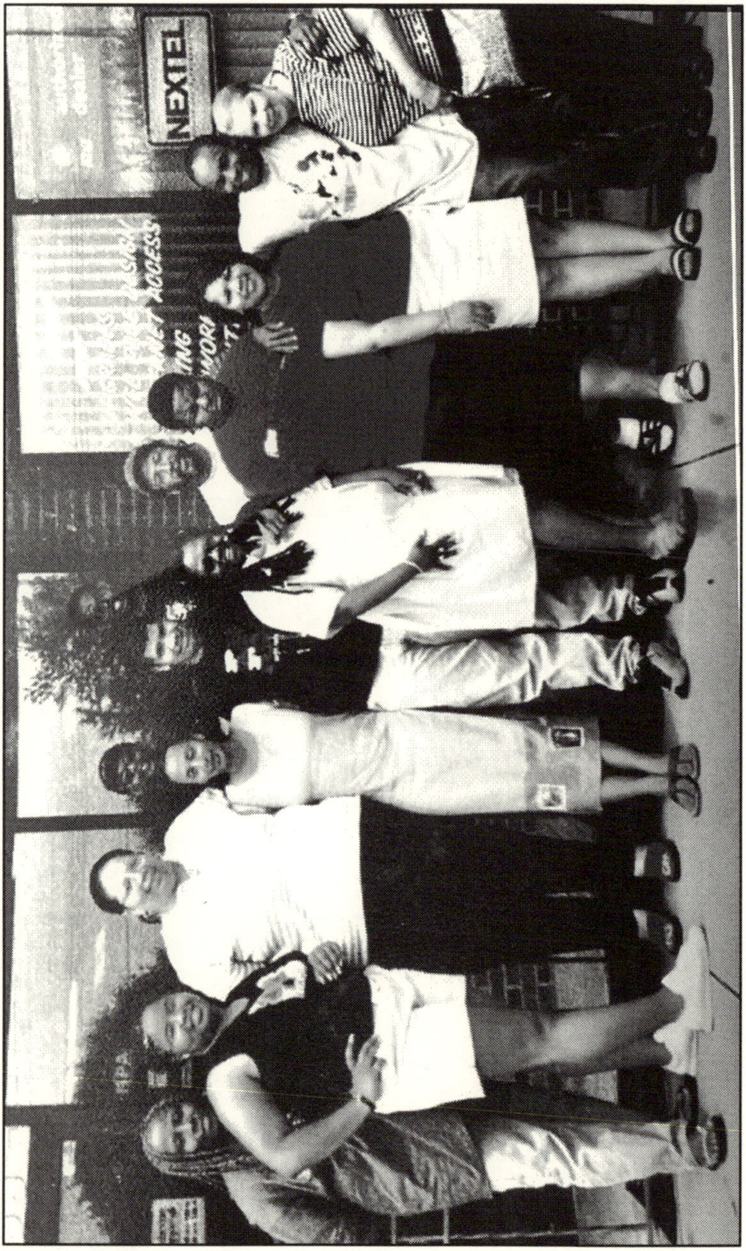
NEXTEL

Family Photo from 2001
(Opposite Page)

Left to Right
P. Thandi Hicks Harper, Thandika Star Harper Hicks Wilson, Belinda Harper, Billo Harper, Fatima Leonard, Robert Lee Harper Jr., Zuri Holmes, Ann Marie Palmer-Harper, Robert Lee Harper Sr., , Tiffani Harper Hodo, Carlin Harper, Doris Harper Allen.

Letters of Support for Doris Harper Allen's Honorary Doctorate

September 19, 2019

To: Arthur T. Dean II
Executive Director for Campus and Community Access and Inclusion
James Madison University

Re: Selection Committee for Honorary Doctor of Doris Harper Allen

Dear Art,

I am writing to nominate Doris Harper Allen for the Honorary "Doctor of Humanities," for her extraordinary service to the Harrisonburg community, and her tremendous generosity and help to JMU students and faculty in numerous classes.

I first met Ms. Allen five years ago when I was putting together a community conversation considering the impact of two Urban Renewal projects on Newtown in the northeast section of Harrisonburg. Many residents suggested I contact her because of her role as both a leader in the community and someone with a deep understanding of the African-American experience in Harrisonburg. She graciously accepted to speak about her experiences on stage in front of 120 of the town's residents. Before and after that event, I interviewed her repeatedly. It quickly became clear that this had been a very difficult time. Officials seized her home using eminent domain and her family had been displaced. Indeed her whole neighborhood, more than 125 houses, businesses, and churches were burned or bulldozed to the ground. But she wasn't bitter and she carefully avoided assigning blame.

She did, however, very much want to tell her story, not just of Urban Renewal, but of her life in Harrisonburg over the past eighty years. And she accomplished that with great honesty and candor first at the community conversation and also in interviews. Frequently in these meetings she would declare, "I need to write my story, I need to write a book." I was encouraging but certainly not persuaded that this would happen. But soon she began writing every day, found an editor and in remarkably little time, her memoir, "The Way It Was, Not the Way It Is" appeared.

This semester I'm teaching a course focusing on Harrisonburg's history and the African-American experience during the 1950s and 1960s. I knew from the time I started planning that her book would be an essential source. It's extremely difficult to find this kind of thoughtful detailed memoir – especially for Harrisonburg. My students also quickly realized the importance of the book. Here is one of them describing it in a journal,

I feel that this book is insanely important due to its first-person account of the African American culture as it was. This book allows for those who hadn't experienced this type of life to get an understanding of the culture. For those of us who are not from Harrisonburg, this book gave us a look into the way things were and how much things have changed. This text ties together the effects of racial and money-based decision making. Since everything was originally segregated, the African American community learned to support themselves without outside help. The text also speaks to the after-effects of integration, which divided the African American-community even more.

It was my conversations with Doris that inspired me to learn more about Harrisonburg's past. And it's for this reason that the book "Picturing Harrisonburg" is dedicated to her. With her calm but forthright manner, she has inspired countless people to speak their own truths. But she has also helped us to understand resilience. Doris is still here, living in Harrisonburg, after all that has happened. And she's still working to make this a better community.

Doris Harper Allen is a model of all three of JMU's stated values of engaged learning and civic and community engagement. Engaged learning: over the last five years she has worked closely with JMU students and faculty, helping us to understand important parts of the history of the place they now call home – important parts that have been left out of the established story, and in the process she has helped to bring campus and community closer together. Community Engagement: Doris has already received 11 different awards from a range of groups in both Harrisonburg and Huntington, West Virginia for her work in this sphere. Civic Engagement: Doris' commitment to civil rights started in the 1940s and continues to this day. It did not surprise me to learn, in one of her conversations, that she took her son out of school on August 28th 1963 and travelled to Washington D.C. because she wanted to be sure he would hear Martin Luther King speak at the March on Washington.

The great majority of James Madison University honorary doctorates have been awarded to politicians: governors, state representatives, and judges. We even bestowed one on former Senator F. Harry Byrd Jr., the architect of massive resistance. It was Byrd's policies that ensured that Ms. Allen would never receive a degree at James Madison University. In place of an education, she was afforded the opportunity to work as JMU as President J. Tyler Miller's cook for several years. Looking at everything she accomplished without higher education, considering her leadership in community engagement and her tremendous generosity to our students and faculty, I can only imagine what she might have achieved, had she been permitted to attend James Madison.

Ms. Allen already meets the award criteria for an Honorary Doctorate through her extensive public service and scholarship. And her life and work align closely with the university's strategic priority of engagement, as the guidelines require. These also state that JMU is "committed to diversity" and "supports the awarding of honorary doctorates that reflect the diversity of interests, backgrounds and opportunities represented in the JMU community." Since 1983, only six of these doctorates have been conferred on women, and only four on African Americans. If the award criteria actually reflect our values, our commitments, and our priorities, then there is no better candidate for this degree than Doris Harper Allen.

Should you have any questions about Ms. Allen or this nomination, please do not hesitate to contact me.

David Ehrenpreis
Director, Institute for Visual Studies
Professor, History of Art

Dr. Mollie Godfrey
Department of English
Keezell 215, MSC 1801
James Madison University

Dr. Sean McCarthy
School of Writing, Rhetoric & Technical Communication
Harrison 2265, MSC 2103
James Madison University

March 1, 2018

Re: Honorary Doctorate for Doris Harper Allen

Dear Selection Committee,

We are writing to ask you to consider presenting Doris Harper Allen with an honorary doctorate from James Madison University. We believe that Doris is an outstanding candidate for this award, as she has been a tireless advocate for the African American community in Harrisonburg as a writer, activist, and community leader.

We first got to know Doris through our work on "Celebrating Simms: The Story of the Lucy F. Simms School," an ongoing university/community partnership that has resulted in a permanent exhibit in the Lucy F. Simms Center for Continuing Education in Harrisonburg. That exhibit, which opened in May 2016, has since been installed in all of the Harrisonburg and Rockingham County high schools, and has been the recipient of several local and national awards and grants (see the "Celebrating Simms" website, https://omeka.jmu.edu/simms/ for more information.)

Doris was a key figure in making the "Celebrating Simms" project a reality. Her first book, *The Way It Was, Not The Way It Is* (2015), was a key text in the syllabus of "Representing Black

Harrisonburg," the course we taught together and that formed the platform from which we co-designed the "Celebrating Simms" exhibit with community partners and JMU students. We cannot overstate Doris' importance in anchoring the project in authentic community dialogue and exchange. She became a bridge between the community and the university, with her involvement and charismatic support quickly drawing other members of the community into the project. She visited with the students on several occasions throughout the academic year to read from her book, provide context for the students' ongoing research, identify individuals in photographs, and offer substantive and valuable feedback on drafts of student work. She was generous with providing documents and photographs from her personal archive, as well as anecdotes and encouragement to the students throughout the entire process. It is often difficult for students to fully appreciate the complexity and richness of a community's history. Doris's unique voice (in both speech and writing) provided them with an anchor as they developed their research and tried to articulate the nuance and historical significance of education to the African American community in Harrisonburg and beyond.

It is also worth noting that when Doris graduated from the Lucy F. Simms School in 1945, attending university at what was then Madison College was not an option, as the college remained segregated until 1966. Instead of being able to pursue her dream of becoming a historian, Doris took the work that was available to her as an African American woman in the segregated south. It was not until the age of 88 that she was finally able to fulfill that early dream on her own time. *The Way It Was, Not The Way It Is* is the only memoir of African American life in Harrisonburg during segregation. Doris's second book, *Jim Crow*, which she wrote at the age of 90, digs even deeper into the harsh realities of life for local African Americans at that time. Along with her first book, both will be essential sources for our students as we continue to grow the "Celebrating Simms" project, and both will be key resources for the local high schools as they continue to expand their local history curricula (see Rockingham County Public School's

Chapters of Rockingham website, http://localhistory.rockingham.k12.va.us/ for more information).

In our experience as teachers and community engagement practitioners, we understand all too well the difficulty of doing justice to the diversity and richness of a community, particularly one that has been under-represented. People like Doris are not just vital collaborators that provide forward motion for projects, they are inspirational figures who encourage us to be our best engaged selves. Doris's self-driven commitment to education and engagement—undeterred by the serious challenges of segregation— exemplify the university's mission. We recommend her for this honor without hesitation.

> Sincerely,
> Dr. Mollie Godfrey and
> Dr. Sean McCarthy

Dr. Kevin L. Borg
Department of History
58 Bluestone Drive MSC 2001
James Madison University

Dear Director Dean,

I would like to offer my strong support for the nomination of Doris Harper Allen to the Honorary Doctor of Humanities at James Madison University. Her description of the black experience in Harrisonburg during her lifetime shows the innate skills of a natural historian. Her book, *The Way it Was, Not the Way it Is*, provided the Harrisonburg and JMU community a critically needed corrective to the older historical narratives of the community by professional historians such as John Wayland. Her forthcoming book on Jim Crow, which I have had the opportunity to see in the early draft stages, promises to be an equally important contribution.

When I embarked on teaching a public history workshop focused on Harrisonburg in 2007, my students and I sensed a gaping hole in the published histories of the city. The history of the twentieth century was sparse, but the history of the African-American community during that time even more so. It was not until years later that I finally met Ms. Allen at one of the regular monthly "Memory Days" at Simms School, organized by Robyn Lyttle, of the Shenandoah Valley Black History Project. Ms. Allen is the kind of community treasure that professional historians are delighted to meet—they know where the bodies are buried, so to speak. She would not have been accepted into the Normal School at Harrisonburg to train to be a historian. But she has trained herself to be one, to be a record-keeper, a writer, and a voice for the history of *her* community. She has been exceptionally generous in sharing her time and expertise with myself, other faculty, and the students we guide in local research projects. Without her contributions, my students' understanding of what inclusive, engaged, community history entails would be incomplete. Doris Harper Allen has built a legacy for the Harrisonburg and JMU community that is worthy of the prestigious recognition conferred by the Honorary Doctor of Humanities.

If I may be of further help as you consider Ms. Allen's nomination, please do not hesitate to contact me.

    Sincerely,
    Dr. Kevin Borg

Made in the USA
Middletown, DE
18 February 2023